"Although I have lived with quadriplegia for over half a century, I do not consider myself an expert on dealing with disability, as there are always new challenges. But demanding challenges force me and people like J. D. Kim to lean hard into the grace of God for every need. In his new book, *From Walking to Wheeling*, my friend poignantly shares how every weakness can become a platform for the power of God's grace to be displayed."

—Joni Eareckson Tada
Founder and CEO, Joni and Friends International Disability Center

"In *From Walking to Wheeling*, J. D. Kim recounts his remarkable and painful adventure of the past eighteen years. I have known Kim since he sustained his spinal cord injury, rendering him a quadriplegic in 2004, and I have witnessed his unfaltering perseverance and hard work, which resulted in numerous scholarships. I am so grateful for Kim's story, which is a living theology as the result of a lived theology. It has been such an inspiration to me and will be such an encouragement to others."

—Stephanie Percival
Retired director of clinical care management, Craig Hospital

"Not everyone largely paralyzed in a major skiing accident comes back to complete master's and doctoral degrees and goes on to teach as an adjunct and assistant director at an alma mater. Very few manage to live a life in which they can honestly say they rejoice in their circumstances because of their relationship with Jesus Christ. J. D. Kim has done all of this and writes his story in a very down-to-earth, emotion-packed, and page-turning style. I recommend it to the widest possible cross-section of readers."

—Craig L. Blomberg
Professor emeritus of New Testament, Denver Seminary

"This book is a treasure. J. D. Kim did not waste his sufferings. Instead, he turned wounds into a pearl. He believed in God who writes a drama of reversal through sufferings. I highly recommend this book to anyone looking to gain a deeper understanding of God's providence for the broken ones."

—Choon-min Joshua Kang
Author of *Deep-Rooted in Christ*

"This book is full of divine inspiration, invincible hope, and unquenchable longing for God's ultimate victory and vindication. J. D. Kim's testimony is a must-read for anyone that is struggling with pain, suffering, disability, vanity, and meaninglessness in life. This is truly one of the most powerful and amazing stories of healing and restoration available today."

—Sung Wook Chung
Professor of Christian theology, Denver Seminary

"In *From Walking to Wheeling*, J. D. Kim has given us a deeply personal, honest account of suffering and the loving God who meets us in that suffering. He does not hold back from anything—the pain, the doubts, the fears, the frustrations, the humiliation, the hypocrisy, and the anger of why me!? For those who have wondered about that same question, this is a testimony that will truly inspire."

—Suzanne Scholte
Seoul Peace Prize laureate

"J. D. Kim writes from the heart and to the heart. His story is a powerful one of grief, loss, pain, suffering, redemption, salvation, recovery, and glory. The way he finds hope even amidst the brokenness of his condition offers inspiration to all of us who would follow in the footsteps of Jesus and offer our lives as living sacrifices. This book is for anyone looking for hope in the midst of hopelessness. Joy in the midst of great suffering. Peace in the midst of anxiety and fear."

—Doug Resler
Senior pastor, Parker Evangelical Presbyterian Church

"Life in this complicated, broken world takes from us all it can. In this book, J. D. Kim reflects on his path, and on the amazing provision our God offers to us, divine power which enables ordinary people to thrive amidst the ruts and rocks. Wrapped in wisdom and gratitude, Kim is a godly man finding the stamina and grace to help us all finish well."

—Brad Strait
Senior pastor, Cherry Creek Presbyterian Church

"J. D. Kim tells a heart wrenching story of tragedy, struggle, perseverance, and hope. With his life laid bare, Kim allows the reader to walk inside his life experience and see the love of God in new ways. This book will challenge and inspire you to make the most out of the life you've been given."

—Curt Taylor
Senior pastor, Cherry Hills Community Church

"If you are like me and appreciate an honest memoir that tells you not just the story of a life changed, but that also reminds you of our faithful God, then you will enjoy J. D. Kim's heart moving book."

—Kelly M. Kapic
Author of *You're Only Human*

"*From Walking to Wheeling* recounts an inspirational journey from self-centered to God-centered living, from anxiety to freedom, from sorry to joy. J. D. Kim's autobiographical account of his tragic snowboarding accident and resulting paralysis poignantly captures intense moments of frustration, fear, and anger as he wrestles with his new reality. Everyone who has faced devastating life-changing circumstances will be uplifted and encouraged by his wise words of grace."

—Lynn H. Cohick
Provost and dean of academic affairs, Northern Seminary

"J. D. Kim knows about suffering, and he knows about loving Jesus. For some, these two things do not go together. But for Kim, his story, described in this book, led him to make a decision to love Jesus that not only reshaped his life in the face of suffering but is impacting all the people that he speaks to, teaches, or anyone who read his words. I am amazed and blessed by his story and his heart for Jesus."

—Brad Meuli
President and CEO, Denver Rescue Mission

"In this bracingly honest memoir, J. D. Kim shows us the many ways in which acquired quadriplegia challenges both its recipient and the church—without quieting the voice of the God who desires every Christian to be a conduit of his love. A riveting and poignant tale of a journey out of a life oriented by self-centered dreams into a living conversation with a God who gives wholly new and lifegiving dreams."

—Brian Brock
Professor of moral and practical theology, University of Aberdeen

"*From Walking to Wheeling* is a remarkable story of J. D. Kim's agonizing journey in finding his purpose in life after a snowboarding accident left him a quadriplegic in constant pain and totally dependent upon others for his care. Kim hit bottom and cried out to God, and he gained confidence and strength in him. Through this painful journey, he found the purpose for his life is to glorify God and not to receive something from him."

—Steven G. Stirling
President and CEO, MAP International

From Walking *to* Wheeling

From Walking *to* Wheeling

How God Reconstructed One Man's Dreams

J. D. KIM

Foreword by Gary Thomas

RESOURCE *Publications* · Eugene, Oregon

FROM WALKING TO WHEELING
How God Reconstructed One Man's Dreams

Copyright © 2023 J. D. Kim. All rights reserved. Except for brief quotations in critical publications or reviews, no part of this book may be reproduced in any manner without prior written permission from the publisher. Write: Permissions, Wipf and Stock Publishers, 199 W. 8th Ave., Suite 3, Eugene, OR 97401.

Resource Publications
An Imprint of Wipf and Stock Publishers
199 W. 8th Ave., Suite 3
Eugene, OR 97401

www.wipfandstock.com

PAPERBACK ISBN: 978-1-6667-6676-9
HARDCOVER ISBN: 978-1-6667-6677-6
EBOOK ISBN: 978-1-6667-6678-3

VERSION NUMBER 030923

All Scripture quotations, unless otherwise indicated, are taken from the Holy Bible, New International Version®, NIV®. Copyright ©1973, 1978, 1984, 2011 by Biblica, Inc.™ Used by permission of Zondervan. All rights reserved worldwide. www.zondervan.com. The "NIV" and "New International Version" are trademarks registered in the United States Patent and Trademark Office by Biblica, Inc.™

To my God who holds me with his righteous right hand;
my parents who sacrifice their life for me;
my family who makes themselves available for my needs;
my friends who love me as I am;
my mentors who encourage and guide me to dream God's dreams;
and my ministry partners whose support and prayer move me

Some names, places, businesses, and details have been changed to protect their privacy.

Contents

Foreword by Gary Thomas | ix

Preface | xiii

Part 1: My Dreams | 1

Part 2: Broken Body | 15

Part 3: My Life at Craig Hospital | 24

Part 4: Broken Life | 41

Part 5: New Life with God | 53

Part 6: New Dream | 102

Epilogue | 119

Foreword

Clarence Macartney, a prominent pastor in the first half of the twentieth century, spoke of modern-day prodigals who leave their homes in search of something better. "You can find him in Pittsburgh, you can find him in Rome, you can find him in Athens; you can find him yesterday, today, and tomorrow. Always the experiment has the same dismal ending. . . . How merciless the world is to those who worship it! How cruel it is to those who love it!"[1] These desperate souls are those who "are trying to get more out of the world than there is in it."[2]

That once described J. D. Kim, a sushi chef who had little interest in the things of God as he pursued what he thought was his life's calling. While making sushi *excited* him, it didn't *fulfill* him. He plunged deeply into addictive behavior, which you'll read about here. As soon as a snowboarding accident immobilized him physically, J. D. started to come alive spiritually, literally reciting the Lord's Prayer as he waited for the ski patrol to get him down from the mountain.

Months and then years of hospital stays and treatments, hours of unanswered prayer, led J. D. to a dark place through which he could finally see the light. "I was completely broken in every way. My confidence and hope of walking were shattered into a million pieces without any possibility of repair. I was finally awake from my fantasy and faced the cruel reality for the first time since the accident. I thought I was dreaming a nightmare, but the reality was worse."

At first, J. D. fell into the same trap all of us do at one time or another: seeking something from God instead of God himself. "I was so focused on receiving what I wanted that my relationship with him became focused on

---

1. Clarence E. Macartney, *Sermons from Life* (Nashville: Cokesbury, 1933), 48–50.
2. Macartney, *Sermons from Life*, 51.

his healing and powerful hands, and neglected to seek his face . . . I mistook God for a genie in a lamp, thinking that if I rubbed the lamp hard and long enough, he would come out and grant my wishes."

We will never be satisfied by a genie. We can only be satisfied by God.

Shorn of every other comfort, J. D. found a new delight in reaching out to God. What he found surprised him: the spiritual joys he had despised in his childhood were in fact superior joys as he grew in the Lord. "I began to experience joy in reading and reflecting on his words and spending time with him. It was a joy that I had never experienced before. It was different from the pleasures of the world, going to parties and on vacations, playing golf or hanging out with friends. Sometimes the joy felt like fireworks of dopamine filling every part of my body, soul, and spirit in perfect balance. I was often so fully immersed in the presence of God that I wanted to dwell in that moment for the rest of my life and wanted time and the world to stop."

J. D. was finding out that God was enough to satisfy him. "I had never understood the psalmist when he said that the word of God was sweeter than honeycomb; I thought he was exaggerating. I was wrong. The psalmist did not go far enough in describing the joy of reflection on God's words. It was truly a miracle. I used to think that the Christian life without any drugs or alcohol was boring and I could not understand the smiles and happy faces of my parents and church members. Yet I became another fool in Christ."

J. D. couldn't shift his circumstances—to this day he is still in a chair that needs to be elevated every fifteen minutes to prevent sores. But he could shift his attention to the God who is good enough for him, and that has been his salvation and his joy.

I see J. D. at church almost every Sunday, and I'm reminded to lift up my soul to the God who truly satisfies. Most of us are still giving the world a try, still thinking there must be more to it that can satisfy us. We put maybe half our hope in God, at best. Half our pleasure in walking in his presence. Half our fulfillment in receiving from him. J. D. found that when he was forced to put all his hope in God, the promise and allure of the world melted as fast as a late spring snow.

Without discovering the spiritual wealth that J. D. knows about, we are like children fighting over dirty pennies when God is covering fields with golden nuggets that lie ignored and unappreciated. J. D. calls us to find our hope, joy, satisfaction, and delight in the only thing that truly satisfies, a vibrant relationship with God. The NLT translates Jesus's promise in John 10:10 as "My purpose is to give them a rich and satisfying life." God's first command in the Garden of Eden was to "eat freely" and in the New Testament he urges us to "be filled" (Eph 5:18). Eat freely, Adam and Eve! Be filled with the Spirit, Christian! The Bible begins and ends with a call to abundance. Why settle for anything less than what Paul prays for the Ephesians, that we "may be filled to the measure of all the fullness of God" (Eph 3:19).

I am grateful to J. D. for writing such a heart-wrenching memoir that calls us to experience the fullness of God. You hold in your hands a testimony to joy in the face of suffering and a declaration that spiritual treasures and life in Christ are superior to any other life or any other pleasure this world might offer.

Gary Thomas
December 2022

Preface

BEING AN IMMIGRANT FROM *South Korea, writing a book was never a part of my dream. If it had been, it would certainly not have been about the humiliation and brokenness I experienced after a snowboarding accident left me paralyzed when I was twenty-two years old. Nor could I ever have imagined using a typing stick on each of my hands in order to write a book that describes my unexpected and life-changing experiences caused by the accident.*

Being paralyzed from my shoulders down, my dreams seemed too shattered to be restored. My identity, self-esteem, and mind were all broken to the point where I gave up believing in myself. I hated myself without empathy, forgiveness, and love, and I could not accept the new version of myself. In this state of brokenness, my new journey as a quadriplegic began. I searched for healing through science, medicine, and religion. Gradually, the journey became one of experiencing God's grace through both suffering and miracles, unanswered and answered prayers, and spiritual and emotional ups and downs, until I was finally pursuing the dreams that God wanted me to dream as a result of my relationship with him.

I want "authenticity" to be a primary characteristic of this book because it speaks to the hearts of people. To that end, I penned somewhat detailed descriptions of experiences I regret, and take no pride in, that occurred both before and after my accident. I also share frankly about God's faithful hand on my life. One friend suggested that I should not talk about God in this book in order to reach a broader audience. But God has been so deeply involved in my life that if I left him out of it, the story would only tell half of the truth. I cannot be what I am today without his involvement. I shared specific stories that unfolded in those years, including my interpretations of the stories and personal reflections, hoping that you could walk alongside me through my journey and feel what I felt as you read the story. This book unfolds in real time through six themes and parts: my old dreams, my broken body, my life at Craig Hospital, my broken life, my new life with God, and my new dreams. This book ends with an epilogue in which I provide my theological interpretation of the snowboarding accident.

This is not just one man's story. Even though the degree of suffering can be felt and dealt with differently by individuals, all people experience suffering in one form or another whether physically, emotionally, spiritually, financially, relationally, politically, or culturally. Simultaneously, suffering can impact our health, emotions, spirit, dreams, plans, careers, identities, self-esteem, confidence, hope, lifestyle, attitude, appearance, worldview, religion, purpose, values, and even our relationships with family, friends, and God. In this way, although you may not suffer the hardship and discomfort of living with a severe disability, you have experienced suffering in other forms. Therefore, regardless of our differences and backgrounds, we are connected to each other through the experience of suffering; we struggle to be liberated from it and to find nothing but happiness for our loved ones and for ourselves. Let this story be the story of a neighbor and fellow human being struggling to survive and thrive while living in this broken and unfair world.

My testimonial could be viewed as self-praise or boastful of my deeds and efforts. For instance, you might think that because I did x, y, and z, and received a, b, and c, that if you do them you will receive God's blessing as well. Yes, I want God's blessing over you but I do not believe that God always uses the same tactics to accomplish what he desires in each of our lives. However, I truly and honestly want to brag about my God who has been walking with me on the rocky road, pushing my wheelchair from behind, pulling it from the front, and bearing my suffering with me. This God loved me so much that he has suffered and died for me on the cross and gave his life for my life to accomplish his glorious plans for me. I love him very much.

I also want to share about my parents who, in their Christ-like love, have sacrificed their time, strength, and lives for their only child. Since the accident they have continued walking the walk with me, being patient with me without forcing me to move on with my life, and providing me with financial, physical, and spiritual support, just as they have from the moment I was born. They are not just caregivers; they are ministry partners and friends and like a brother and sister in Christ. As their son, they are the best parents ever; as a believer, they are my role models of faith; as my ministry partners, they are the most loyal and trustworthy; as fellow human beings, I respect them highly; as one receiving care, they are the most reliable caregivers. I want to celebrate and acknowledge the love of many parents around the world who struggle to believe in and love their children at all costs and to express my gratitude for all the caregivers who freely and often necessarily take care of their loved ones. Taking care of family members is easier said than done, and I recognize that not all people are blessed with having such supportive, loving parents.

I write this book for my brothers and sisters struggling with various suffering around this messed-up world that is filled with inequality, injustice, suffering, discrimination, evil, immorality, poverty, hunger, sex-trafficking, racism, wars, crime, natural disasters, suicide, disability, and selfishness. I hate every form of suffering and feel pain when I think about your suffering and its influence on you. I recognize how hard it is to endure and live with suffering (especially chronic pain), to hide your suffering for the sake of your loved ones, to overcome the temptation to be identified, controlled, and trapped by suffering, and to share your suffering with others. I have no intention of sugarcoating suffering and its potential outcome for something better. Rather, I have every intension of telling you that God loves you. I cannot say that if you come to God all your challenges will be resolved and evaporate as if they never existed, but I can tell you with confidence that we can laugh together, hope again, and dream freely in Jesus Christ.

As one of my professors taught me, I believe that if we can share, we can bear. If we can share our suffering together, we can bear it together. If we can share our suffering with Jesus, we can bear it with him. Therefore, I am sharing my suffering and vulnerability. My prayer is that this book may serve as a springboard for encouraging fellow sufferers to experience and get to know the God who meets us in our suffering. I also pray that sharing my brokenness and weakness may encourage those of you who might be going through suffering in whatever shape that may it be; suffering is suffering.

Part 1

My Dreams

I lay on the fresh powder, slowly realizing that something was gravely wrong. Just moments earlier I had been snowboarding down the mountain; now my body was motionless. December 13, 2004, became the dividing line that separated my life into two distinct parts: "before" and "after." Before that fateful day I was an aspiring sushi chef with big dreams and a bright future. I lived a worldly lifestyle. I rarely thought about God. But that one moment on that one day changed everything for me. Over time, God slowly revealed to me a new dream that was bigger and brighter than anything I had ever dared to dream before.

How My Dreams Began

As a young adult I had many dreams. They were not big dreams like Martin Luther King Jr.'s, but rather simple dreams to live a happy life. I wanted to party with my friends, drink alcohol, and get high on drugs. I wanted to visit popular tourist destinations and Michelin starred restaurants around the world. I also wanted to marry the love of my life; live in a big house near the ocean with a swimming pool, hot tub, and remodeled basement with a mini-bar, pool table, and movie screen; drive fancy cars and motorcycles; and have three or four children because I was often lonely growing up as an only child. My dreams also included taking cruise vacations, buying a vacation home in South Korea, and supporting my parents so they would not have to work in their sixties. Many successful individuals were already living my dreams, and thinking about doing these things made me happy and motivated me to dream more and work harder. I was certain that they would make me happy. I could not understand how some people, particularly Christians like my parents, could live happily without drinking and doing drugs, like I did.

It took some time, but I realized that in order to accomplish my dreams, I needed to figure out a way to make a lot of money. I decided that I would become a businessowner and open a high-end Asian-fusion restaurant. I planned to achieve these goals by working as a sushi chef, saving money, opening a small restaurant, finding business investors, and finally starting a high-end restaurant. Over the years, these ideas were developed through meeting people with similar dreams, but it was choosing to become a sushi chef that instigated all of my plans. Becoming a sushi chef was not my parents' idea of achieving the American dream. They immigrated to the United States from South Korea when I was thirteen and worked hard to give me an opportunity to receive the best education in the world. So how did I decide that becoming a sushi chef would be the key to realizing my dreams?

I Like Sushi

I discovered the passion to become a sushi chef when I was about sixteen years old. My friend Jong worked at a Japanese restaurant as a sushi helper, and one day he asked if I would help with washing dishes for a few days after school. I had never worked at a restaurant before and hadn't even washed dishes at home, but I agreed to help him out. When we found out that the restaurant no longer needed help washing dishes, the owner asked whether I would be interested in assisting the sushi chefs by running errands and cleaning the sushi bar for a few days. Jong assured me that he would make me sushi rolls and sushi, which my parents couldn't afford. So I said, "I am in!"

As promised, Jong made me sushi and sushi rolls. I realized why people spend so much money on them. The chefs taught me how to make sushi rolls such as California Rolls and Spicy Tuna Rolls which are basic dishes in Japanese restaurants. I discovered that making a sushi roll was very similar to making a traditional Korean dish, *Gimbap*, which Mom often made for my family. At the restaurant I made a Japanese version of *Gimbap* by paying attention to the chefs, and actually enjoyed the new experiences.

I later learned that becoming a sushi chef could be extremely difficult in many ways. Depending on the needs of the sushi chefs, it could take weeks for an intern sushi chef or sushi helper to learn how to make sushi rolls and months to learn how to make sushi. If the chefs had learned their Japanese culinary skills the hard way, some of them gave newbies a hard time. And if the owner or head chef of a Japanese restaurant pursued high-quality Japanese cuisine, interns had to start by washing dishes and handling vegetables and food preparation before they could learn to make the most basic of Japanese cuisine: sushi rice.

Jong and his coworkers taught me how to make sushi rolls that week without making it difficult for me. I enjoyed working at the Japanese restaurant because not only did I get to eat Japanese food, but I also got to drink *sake* with the chefs who loved to drink, even during work when customers at the sushi bar bought them drinks. After helping them for one week, the owner of the restaurant mentioned that the chefs saw potential in me and offered me an opportunity be an intern sushi helper (they probably needed extra help). Although I wanted to accept the opportunity, I was on probation and required to attend high school and could not take a full-time job.

At seventeen I dropped out of high school and received my GED. I passed it without having taken many classes during high school. In South Korea, the GED represents a high standard, so it is possible that my parents were under the false impression that their son was smart enough to succeed in college. Dad was an educator and pastor and believed that receiving an education was the best option for my future. He insisted I attend college, even though I'd gotten in trouble at school numerous times and skipped classes throughout high school. Knowing that Dad would kick me out of the house, I reluctantly started what seemed like a meaningless journey at Arapahoe Community College. I had to pay the expensive out-of-state tuition because I was living in the US with a student visa. "What a waste," I thought.

My old habit of skipping classes continued in college as I was more interested in finding a part-time job to make money to enjoy my life with my friends. But there were a few obstacles to getting a job. First, as my driver's license was suspended before I turned eighteen, I needed to find a job near my house. Second, I needed a part-time job that paid cash. Because of the nature of my student visa (F-2), I was not allowed to work in the US legally. There were only few places that were willing to violate the law to pay workers in cash. Lastly, I had to help dad's ministry on Saturday evenings, so my availability was limited.

During the long job search, I found a small Japanese teriyaki restaurant less than five minutes away by bike that was hiring a waiter. The owner of the business liked me and gave me a part-time job despite the above disadvantages. After working there for two or three days, the owner learned that I had worked as a sushi helper for a short time. He instantly promoted me to sushi helper.

At the restaurant I met Tom, a Korean sushi chef who was kind and gentle. He was so happy to finally have a Korean helper with whom he could converse in Korean, since most of the Korean employees working at the restaurant could not speak Korean well. On the first day of working as a sushi helper, he asked me to make a California Roll. But by then, I had already forgotten how to make it and was not prepared for such a test; it looked terrible. Surprisingly, he did not mind at all, and started training me as his apprentice and helper and teaching me the basics such as making sushi rice, cutting vegetables, and setting up and cleaning the sushi bar. Learning to make sushi and filleting fish could take months, perhaps even a year, depending on the personality and mindset of the sushi chefs in charge of training helpers. Tom told me that he learned his skills the hard way and spent many years working as a sushi helper before becoming a sushi chef. He hated it so much that he would not make it hard for me. Thanks to Tom, I was able to learn the skills quickly and got better every day.

Unfortunately, as business slowed, I had to be let go. I found another Japanese restaurant and worked there for one or two months but lost my job again because the owner needed a full-time employee who could work on Saturdays and receive legal paychecks. I was willing to pay taxes and even work for a minimum wage, but because I had an F-2 visa and later an R-2 visa (religious visa), I could not work legally in this country. Disappointment, bitterness, and anger filled my heart. Dad tried to encourage me. "As you know," he told me, "I have an R-1 visa right now and will be able to submit an application for a Green Card in a few months or a year. When it gets approved, you will have the legal status to work wherever you want when you are around twenty or so. Be patient." Waiting for four more years seemed like an eternity, but I had no choice but to wait.

My Relationship with God

Although I was not interested in living a Christian life and accepting its values, my Christian "résumé" began in South Korea. I was born and raised in a Christian family. I went to church every Sunday, participated in Bible studies and on the church worship team, and attended vacation Bible studies, revival services, seminars, and so forth. I participated in these church activities not because I was a faithful Christian, but because my Christian parents forced me to do them.

Unlike my parents, who willingly served their church, I was involved with church activities for two reasons. First, Dad was a youth pastor of the church that we attended, and pastor's kids (PKs) were expected to be part of their parents' ministries. The second and main reason was that he held conservative Korean values on disciplining and raising children. That is a nice way of saying that spanking was an acceptable form of discipline. He kicked my butt when I caused troubles at school, so skipping any church activities was unimaginable. In fact it was so imaginable that I always participated in church activities, though unwillingly and reluctantly.

The only time I was passionate about participating was when I wanted to join a worship team to play the guitar to impress a girl. I bought a book on playing the guitar and practiced every day. Sadly, we remained "just friends." But then I couldn't quit the worship team because I was afraid of Dad. Later, when I was about seventeen years old, I played the drums for a non-profit organization that he founded to serve Korean young adults and which supported Aurora Korean Baptist Church (AKBC).

Even after many years of participating in church programs, I was not a fully converted Christian and chose to live a worldly lifestyle. Many of the church programs that Dad led were on Saturdays, so my friends and I gathered at church, participated in church programs, and then went out afterward to party. On Sundays, after attending worship services, we went behind the church to smoke, and then came back smelling like cigarettes. I guess knowing that he could not stop me from hanging out with my friends—though for years he did try using various means—Dad thought that it was better for me to live a worldly lifestyle after doing the church activities. There were a few times when I actively engaged in prayer and discipleship training and repented of sinning against God, but my efforts lasted only about a week or month at best.

Did I believe that going to church on Sunday and playing the drums was like buying an indulgence? Was I a false Calvinist who could sin all

I wanted and still be saved near the end of my life when I said the magic words because I somehow and somewhat (miraculously and skeptically) believed that Jesus was my Savior without demonstrating my faith through good works? Was I brainwashed by many years of Bible studies? Or was I like a lazy Catholic thinking that the prayers and devotions of my parents could save me and cancel my transgressions? Maybe I became a universalist believing that Jesus died for the sins of all people whether people truly accept him or not and whether they live according to the standard of the Bible or not because of the pervasiveness and power of the suffering and death of the Son of God. Perhaps I found a loophole in the concept of God's grace, thinking that as long as I confess with my mouth that Jesus is Lord and ask for his forgiveness, I would be saved, because that is written in the Bible.

A New Opportunity

While attending the community college, I was put on academic suspension because I failed to receive passing grades. Without having to go to school or work, I slept all day, played online games all night, and got high and drunk every day with my friends. But one day I was offered the opportunity to be an apprentice/sushi helper by a man who attended Dad's church. Chris was the head chef at a Japanese restaurant, Yama. He was about thirty-five years old; he had become a sushi chef in his twenties and had already operated a Japanese restaurant in Seattle.

Chris planned to open up a Japanese restaurant in Denver and was so committed that he told the owner that he would train me as his helper and pay me out of his own paycheck. Who would do something like this for someone he barely knew? Dad was moved by Chris commitment to train me and was persuaded that working as a sushi chef could be a good career for me and perhaps eventually present an opportunity to be a business owner, so he finally permitted me to quit college and also allowed me to work on Saturday nights which enabled me to become a full-time sushi helper.

The work schedule was tough. From Monday to Friday, I went to work by 9:00 a.m., prepared for the lunch hours, and took a break at 2:30 p.m. After two hours of a break, I worked from 4:30 p.m. to 10:00 p.m. On Saturday, I worked from 5:30 p.m. to 11:00 p.m., and Sunday was my day off. If customers stayed after the closing hours, I worked longer hours. I worked over sixty hours a week and received $1,000 per month from Chris.

However, I loved working with him because he treated me like his little brother. Because my driver's license was still suspended, he picked me up in the mornings and dropped me off at night. We often drank with co-workers or went to bars after work, and he always paid for everything, telling me that I could pay him back later when I became a sushi chef.

Chris said his customers loved him because he was good looking, but that was not why. I saw how he treated his customers with respect. We would often get drunk with customers who paid for our drinks, and Chris would buy them expensive drinks in return. He did not mind because he was having a great time with his customers who were like friends to him.

Chris always talked about his successful business story when he was drunk, but it still inspired me to be like him. His drunk speeches moved me. He would tell me, "J. D., we are going to open this restaurant together, okay?" He would tell me that we would be successful and that I would have the technique and experience I needed to become a sushi chef in a few years. He would open a second restaurant so we could each have one.

I challenged myself to train harder and study Japanese cooking. Was this the power of someone whom I admired and respected believing in me? Was this the power of having a dream? Could a dream simply start from hearing someone's inspiring, interesting, or exciting story? Once in my own imagination, could I turn the dream into reality?

Unfortunately, the dreams that we talked about shattered when Chris could not buy the Japanese restaurant and he decided to leave Colorado with his family. I regretted not having an appropriate opportunity to express my appreciation for his training and care over the months. Our plans were broken, but I continued following in his footsteps and dreaming our dreams.

After Chris left Colorado, I chose to stay at Yama for the same wage in exchange for being allowed to practice making sushi and to continue learning from other sushi chefs. One of them, John, became my new teacher. He lived near me and gave me a ride to and from work every day. Later, I found out that he and Dad graduated from the same high school in South Korea. Everyone in the restaurant knew that I was paid only $1,000 per month, and they showed me kindness and appreciated my hard work. Even though the long hours of work were challenging, I still enjoyed working there. It was amazing how passionate, committed, and diligent I became to pursue a dream when I did not originally have any plans.

After work, I drank with my co-workers or partied with my friends and got high on drugs like marijuana, coke, and ecstasy; however, I was never late to work or missed a day. During my break times, instead of resting with my coworkers, I practiced making sushi rice balls with the leftover rice without the topping of fish. I made about one hundred sushi rice balls every day in order to make the same size of sushi consistently and tried improving my knife skills using leftover or unusable vegetables. The improvement could save the time in vegetable preparation, and I could ask other chefs for more opportunities to prepare fish, which was the most important and needed skill set for sushi chefs. I studied Japanese words that were related to Japanese cooking and ingredients and found satisfaction in my hard work, despite the low pay, because I had dreams, and my dreams moved me.

Dreaming My Dreams

About ten months later my friend Yo Kung, a professional and recognized sushi chef, offered me the opportunity to work at a fancy new Japanese restaurant which was located near downtown Denver. My friend Tosa allowed me to use his information to work there legally. I paid taxes for him and he did not mind that there was a record of his having worked at a Japanese restaurant.

Working at Shogun Sushi changed the trajectory of my culinary journey. Shogun Sushi is where I met my friend, Akira Back, who is now an influential and renowned chef. At the time he was the head sushi chef at Shogun Sushi. I thought that I was a decent sushi chef but soon realized that Akira was working at a higher level. He taught and challenged me to grow as a chef. When I applied to work at Shogun Sushi, I brought along my friend Sean who has been my friend since high school. He got a job as a sushi helper despite never having worked at a restaurant. We used to be roommates and worked together at a coin laundry and janitorial service company when we were high school students, so we made a good team. Before we started working at Shogun Sushi, I taught Sean how to use knife, prepare vegetables, and make sushi rolls at my house, using newspaper as the seaweed for sushi rolls. I was extremely excited to work at Shogun Sushi, but also worried about working with non-Korean chefs because I was not familiar with the English names for certain ingredients and kitchen

My Dreams

supplies and equipment. However, I felt like all my hard work and training were finally paying off.

The other employees and I invited friends and family members on the opening day of the restaurant. I was excited to show my parents that their troublemaker son was working as a sushi chef for the first time. I wanted to serve my parents the best dishes but knew that my cooking technique was insufficient to impress them, so I asked Akira and the kitchen chefs to prepare their best dishes for them. I contributed *ochazuke*, which is a Japanese soup with rice and other savory ingredients steeped in green tea. I had never made the dish before.

Afterward, I went to my parents' table to talk to them. Dad complimented me on working at a wonderful restaurant and told me he was happy for me. I asked which dish they liked best, hoping that they liked the soup; unfortunately, it was not the soup. "Sorry," Dad said, "That was supposed to be soup? Did you make it?" We all laughed. I was still far from being a good chef, but my parents were delighted and grateful to see me working there and supported my passion to be a sushi chef. They were relieved that I was finally on a positive trajectory in life.

I had a great time working at Shogun Sushi. It was exciting visually and sensually. It turned into a bar near the late-night hours. Many beautiful people, young and old, stopped by to drink and party. My bartender friend hooked me up with scotch and beer each night, and in exchange I made him sushi rolls. After work, our coworker bought Sean and me drinks and we hung out at the restaurant together. We often went to his apartment which was nearby. When we had too much to drink, we crashed there. And there was a bar next to Shogun Sushi where Sean and I joined many servers and chefs to hang out after work. Coke and alcohol were my favorite choices, and I drank almost every day and snorted coke many times a week. Every day was a party for me.

One of the kitchen helpers joined us as a sushi helper and when I found out he was a coke dealer, he became my favorite supplier. Many servers at Shogun Sushi had helpful connections for partying effectively with my friends. Some were bartenders and bouncers at hot clubs, and I got free drinks and access to them through these connections. During my off days, I continued the same pattern of lifestyle. When I met friends who did not do drugs, we either went to restaurants or bars to get drunk or to golf ranges where I would hit a few balls and drink beer. I probably drank six days a week and at least six cans of beer and shots of hard liquor every day.

My body was trained to continue this lifestyle from working at Yama so I was able to maintain my work ethic at the restaurant while simultaneously enjoying my life and improving as a sushi chef.

Matsuhisa

One day, during the team meeting of the sushi bar, Akira asked me if I would be interested in working at Matsuhisa, a Japanese restaurant located in the resort town of Aspen, Colorado. The restaurant was named after a famous Japanese chef, Nobu Matsuhisa. It was a luxurious and boutique Japanese restaurant with franchises in big cities around the world such as New York, Malibu, Beverly Hills, Miami, Milano, Paris, Tokyo, and so forth. Working at such a restaurant was a dream for many sushi chefs if they were ambitious to pursue their career in Japanese cuisine. Once they had experience working at Matsuhisa on their résumé, they could probably get any job—or at least a job interview—at most Japanese restaurants. Having the opportunity to work at Matsuhisa and move to the next level was a dream come true. I needed Matsuhisa on my résumé to prove that I was the real deal. I was all in to move to Aspen and did not hesitate to tell Akira that I would go.

A week after speaking with Matsuhisa's general manager, I went to Aspen with my cousin. The general manager greeted me and introduced me to the head chef. I was nervous and wondered whether or not I should convey confidence. It would appeal to American chefs as strength, but in Asian culture it could be viewed as arrogance. By contrast, taking more of a humble approach could appeal to the Japanese-cultured chef. My head was spinning and confused. Having little experience with interviews, I decided to simply be myself without revealing my visa status.

The interview went well and I was hired. After coming out of the restaurant, I jumped and shouted to my cousin, "I got the f---ing job!" But now I faced the difficult prospect of telling the great news to my parents who wanted me to stay in Denver. It happened so quickly that my parents could not stop me from moving to Aspen but they understood that working at Matsuhisa was a great opportunity and blessed the new journey. I was filled with excitement, passion, and confidence as I came even closer to achieving my dream. I felt like I could do anything.

Within two weeks I was in Aspen and started working at Matsuhisa with more benefits and a higher salary. I received full health care insurance, a ski season pass, employee housing, paid vacation, and daily tips of $150 or more on average during the busy seasons (the summer season from June to August and the winter season from December to March). I had two days off a week and worked from 1:00 p.m. to 11:00 p.m. during the busy seasons. During the off seasons, the town was pretty much empty except for the locals who hung around the town, so the hours were shorter and the work was very easy without any stress and hard work. All things considered, the restaurant offered the best working conditions. I was twenty years old in 2003 and without a college degree or special business hustle or experience, I thought I was doing well.

Working at Matsuhisa was tough at first but amazing. Once again, I was humbled by the techniques and expertise of the Japanese chefs. During the summer and winter seasons, I was able to observe high-level sushi chefs from Japan who came to Aspen and left after the seasons were over. There were other chefs who lived in Aspen who worked there every season, including the executive chef Aku *san* and a sushi chef Sako *san* who were great chefs and had thirty years or more experience of cooking Japanese food. (*San* is a formal title of respect that Japanese people add after the first name. I use the term to show my respect for them). I worked very hard and tried to learn from them as much as possible, taking notes on their work style, preparing sushi rice and fish fillet, making sushi, plating, and using knife, and tried to learn more Japanese words and dishes.

How I Became an Illegal Immigrant

On my twenty-first birthday, unbeknownst to me, I received the most memorable birthday gift: I became an illegal immigrant. A few days after my birthday, Mom called to tell me that I needed to talk to our family immigration lawyer, Tim, about the progress of our Green Card applications which had been submitted several years prior. I talked to him two days later, and what he shared was not good news. His plan was to submit my parents' Green Card application first and to submit my application separately when their application was approved, because he felt that the application process for my parents would go more smoothly without my application and be approved fairly quickly, within a year or two. When their applications were unexpectedly delayed, the lawyer realized he needed to submit mine because I was approaching twenty-one. But by the time my parents' Green

Cards were approved, mine was rejected for further review because I had turned twenty-one.

Tim proceeded to tell me that I had two options to apply for legal status to stay in America. The first option was to apply for a family-based Green Card. My parents would invite me to live here legally and I would apply for a Green Card as an adult child. The issues with this option were that the application process would take a long time and there was no guarantee that I would receive the Green Card. I would also need to go back to South Korea and stay there until the application was accepted. But they did not know whether my application would be approved or how long I would have to wait in Korea. It could be one year, three years, maybe even ten years. My second option, which he characterized as my "final and best way," was to marry an American. He expressed his regrets about the situation. I hung up, went outside, and lit a cigarette.

I knew that there was nothing he could do to revive the dead application. I had been looking forward to having the application approved and finally using my own information to work in this country. (At the time I was using the information of another friend of mine, Gary, to work at Matsuhisa. I told him that it would be temporary, based on the assumption that I would get the Green Card soon. Of course the manager of the restaurant had no idea that I used Gary's information.) I was frustrated. I thought, "Why is it so damn hard to get the Green Card in this country? I already paid thousands of dollars for the application and in legal fees so that eventually I could work and pay taxes legally via the Green Card. Some people are born in this country and have citizenship for free, but although I have done more than them to obtain legal status, I am not qualified to get it because of my age. Well, it is what it is. I cannot change the law. I make a decent amount of money and am good looking. I can probably marry an American citizen or someone with the Green Card if I want one in the future. F--- it. I do not need it right now. I am going to make some money." After dragging on my cigarette bitterly, I went back inside to work.

Dreams Moved Me

My goal for working at Matsuhisa to improve my Japanese cooking skills was clear. But to accomplish this, I needed more opportunities to work in different stations and to earn the respect and approval of my executive chef, for he was the one who assigned the positions and stations of the sushi

My Dreams

chefs. I went to work at least one to two hours before the assigned check-in time for chefs, completed my assigned responsibilities, and tried to help other chefs. The extra hours and effort paid off. I received more opportunities to try different tasks from other chefs. I also volunteered in the kitchen station during my days off to learn more about cooking in general. And I worked at a French fusion restaurant once a week to learn a basic understanding of French cuisine. Although I was not paid during the first season, the owner and head chef of the restaurant offered me a paid part-time position for the second season.

Aku *san* lived in the employee house with me for a few months and we became really close. After work, Aku *san* and I often had BBQ parties for which he prepared the food. He would encourage me and say, "J. D., if you try your best, you can become a head chef someday." Hearing comments like that from a Japanese executive chef at Matsuhisa meant so much to me and perhaps gave me too much confidence. We would drive down to Denver together because I knew the Japanese markets and famous Japanese restaurants. We would also visit my parents on those trips, and Mom would always make my favorite Korean dishes and *Galbi*, which is a Korean BBQ, and pack them in a big icebox. Aku *san* loved Mom's food, especially the soy marinated squid and *Galbi*.

As I was receiving more approval from my executive chef and coworkers, and as my culinary experience and skills were being refined, I could see a vision of my future unfolding. "Things are going well. I am going to work hard and get more experience in Aspen. Maybe in the next year or so I will find a job as a head chef in Los Angeles or Las Vegas, and after a couple years I will find an investor and finally open my own business." I had been saving all my paychecks since I worked at Shogun Sushi, and all my alcohol and drugs were covered by my tips. My life was going well. I enjoyed my life and I was moving closer to realizing my dreams.

New roommates moved into the employment housing after Aku *san* moved out. A sushi helper from Japan, Ten, moved in. He was very respectful and quiet and called me J. D. *san*. Surprisingly, a few months later, my friend Sean—who had continued working with Akira—started working at Matsuhisa, and I was so happy to have him there. Pazu, a Japanese sushi chef who was working at Dojo Sushi located in California, also began living in the employee housing. He was an experienced and talented sushi chef who used to be the head chef at Dojo Sushi, and he loved drinking and partying with me. Even though we often partied together, we were dead serious at work and respected each other, although Pazu did not like Sean very much. Sean and I partied like we had when living in Denver and enjoyed working at the restaurant together. I often gave him my drunken and high "I have a dream" speech, just like Chris used to do.

Deep inside I was struggling with drinking and drugs. For the first several months of living in the employee house with Aku *san*, the executive chef, I drank occasionally and did drugs only when I went to Denver. Thus, I was able to recover physical strength from my previous lifestyle. After Aku *san* left the employee house, I began drinking more often and found a supplier who had the best coke I had ever snorted. Every day was a party when Sean and Pazu became my roommates, though Pazu tried to control himself because of his age. By 2004, I was drinking at least ten cans of beer every day with glasses of hard liquor, snorted coke at least six times a week, smoked weed every day, took a sleeping pill every night, and worked six days a week. My co-workers used to call me a "machine" because I was able to maintain my sharpness at work without looking like I had a hangover. I knew that such a lifestyle could be an obstacle to achieving my dreams but as I was still able to work at a high level without making stupid mistakes, missing work, or being late, I felt no need to give it up. But my body was tired physically. At first I was able to control my lifestyle and give myself some breaks; however, slowly, I lost the ability to control myself and could not stop, although I knew I had to give up my lifestyle to reach my dream. I was like a train without brakes.

Part 2

Broken Body

"Our Father in heaven...." From the deep reaches of my memory I groped for the words of the Lord's Prayer. I did not have a relationship with God, yet I breathed the words I had learned as a child and reached out to him in the only way I knew how at the moment. Those words provided comfort. I could not get up; I could not move. But reciting this prayer was something I could do. It was the only thing, in fact, that I could do.

Two Days before the Accident

Every month or so Sean and I drove the three and a half hours to Denver to buy Korean groceries and food and to meet up with friends and family. The week of December 7, 2004, our days off were the following Sunday and Monday. So we drove to Denver after work on Saturday and planned to drive back to Aspen on Sunday so we could go snowboarding on Monday. We were excited because one of our co-workers told us of the fresh powder and majestic conditions on the mountains. We wanted to snowboard as many times as possible before the restaurant got too busy during the ski season, knowing that we might have to work six days a week. I had been snowboarding since I first moved to Colorado when I was thirteen. I enjoyed taking ski trips with my friends almost every winter. I had decent enough skills to snowboard on black diamond ("expert") trails, although I was not an expert snowboarder like Olympian Sean White.

One Day before the Accident

Back in Denver, that Sunday morning, we attended the Sunday worship service at AKBC, where Dad served as the senior pastor. About seventy people, including my uncle's family, were members of the church, and they had a close relationship with one another. During the summer seasons, the church members played volleyball and soccer with other Korean church teams and ate together after playing games. During holidays like Memorial Day and Labor Day, church members took picnics to mountain and fishing areas to hold outside worship services and to have fellowship with one another. They often filled the whole areas with the aroma of grilled *galbee*. AKBC rented space from a Baptist church associated with Dad's denomination, so everyone had to pitch in to get ready for worship services each Sunday morning. That morning men were busy setting up tables, chairs, instruments, speakers, and mics; women were busy setting up the kitchen to serve the lunch for the congregation; teenagers were busy meeting and connecting with their friends; and children were busy running around the church. Everyone was busy doing something together. Sean and I joined the men getting ready for the worship services.

It was an ordinary worship service. The worship team selected ordinary worship songs, Dad preached an ordinary message, the service proceeded in an ordinary manner, and ordinary church members participated in the Sunday service. Sean and I also participated in the worship service in an ordinary manner.

However, the offering I gave that day was extraordinary, as were my prayers to God. I do not remember the exact amount, but it was much more than I had ever put in the offering bag before. I remember praying to God, "Lord, if you bless me, I will build a church for you. When I open up my business, get married, and settle down, I will live a moral life. Let me enjoy my life for now." I was honest and sincere in my prayer but had no clue where the idea came from. I do not remember whether such a prayer was based on my gratitude for his blessing, desperate need for his help, or arrogance in thinking that putting a few hundred dollars in the offering bag would somehow buy blessings from God. One way or another, it was an extraordinary and random prayer on an ordinary day.

After the worship service Sean and I went to a Korean market to buy groceries, Soju, my favorite Korean wine, and *Kimchi*. As a Korean American born in South Korea and raised by Korean parents, I needed Korean food to survive because Aspen had no Korean markets or restaurants that could satisfy my Korean appetite. We had a couple more stops to make before heading back to Aspen. The first was my parents' house, as Mom wanted to make some Korean food for us. It was already around 6:00 p.m.

My parents were always exhausted on Sunday evenings after a long day of leading the Sunday worship service, small group meetings, and preparing lunch and snack for the congregation. In small churches, the pastor's wife is often in charge of preparing meals for the entire congregation. It is their holy burden and disguised blessing. Mom worked six days a week, and after work on Saturdays she would shop for the groceries she needed to prepare the traditional Korean Sunday lunch fellowship. On that particular Sunday, my parents were not able to catch their breath from the long day until they got home at 5:00 in the evening.

By 7:00 that night, Sean and I were anxious to leave the house. We had planned to meet up with friends before going back to Aspen, and we wanted to have some time to rest before snowboarding the next day. After taking a nap and seeing that my parents were in the kitchen cooking Korean food, I asked them if the food was ready. "Son, I am really tired today," Mom said. "If you sleep at home tonight and leave tomorrow, that will give us extra time to prepare the food. Can you leave tomorrow?" I felt really bad for them, knowing how hard my parents work on Sundays. I asked Sean to go outside to smoke a cigarette, then suggested that we could sleep at my parents' house and leave in the morning. He was against it.

"No, we already planned it. If we do not go snowboarding tomorrow, we may not get to snowboard on fresh snow again this season. Besides, we may not go snowboarding often this season if the restaurant gets really busy." Sean's response was somewhat unusual. He had been one of my best friends since high school. Whenever we disagreed, I usually had the final say and he always supported my decision. However, that evening he was determined to go snowboarding the next day. I did not fully understand how tired my parents were; if I had truly known, I would have convinced Sean to stay there for the night.

Feeling badly for my parents yet wanting to have fun with my friends, I told them that we would head out and that I could pick up the food the next time I was home. "Just rest, please. Don't feel bad." I thought this would resolve the issue, but I was naïve to think that my parents would simply stop cooking and allow me to leave without the food. Mom insisted we wait one more hour saying, "I am almost done." This was not the response I expected but she moved faster to finish cooking my favorites without taking a break after we agreed to wait another hour.

Finally, we left and headed to the next destination where friends from high school welcomed us to their table. We had not seen each other for a long time. Since we were drinking and having a great time together, they asked Sean and me to have more drinks and stay over at our friend Josh's house. Again, I was game, but Sean was unwavering in his intention of driving to Aspen that night. Again I tried to change his mind, but he was so adamant that we almost had a fight. I reluctantly agreed and we drove back to Aspen that night.

The Day

The next day, December 13, 2004, was beautiful. It was cold but sunny with blue skies; it was a perfect day to go snowboarding with friends. Asa, one of our coworkers, joined us and we headed to Aspen Snowmass ski resort. Asa and Sean excitedly told me about a trail that they had found about a week earlier which led to the top of the mountain, so I had them lead the way. After an hour of snowboarding and searching for the trail, they could not find it and I was growing annoyed by their confusion and suggested that we forget about the trail. Eventually, however, they led us to the trail at the top area of the mountain.

I was on the highest place of all the ski resorts that I had ever been on since I started snowboarding in Colorado. As I sat and looked around, the view was breathtaking; the sky was as blue as the ocean; the surrounding mountains were clothed with snow and shining as the sun beamed down on them; the sky was very close to me. I could see the tops of the mountains without having to lift my head and felt like I was at the top of the world.

I found myself getting sentimental when all of a sudden I felt a weird chilling sensation that I had never experienced before; it was a sense that this could be the last time I would be where I was to snowboard on this mountain. It was not quite fear, but it was close to anxiety—it was a bit more intense; perhaps it was an ominous feeling. Something felt off, but I was not sensitive to my gut feeling. Ignoring the sensation, I glided down the snowy mountain.

After about ten or fifteen minutes passed by I stopped and sat on the snow to wait for my friends. I called Dad to see how he was doing, remembering Mom telling me that he had some church issues on his mind. He told me that he felt okay and was in a meeting. After getting up, I lit a cigarette, took a few deep drags, and continued down the mountain. I saw a small mogul and momentarily considered whether to go over or around it. When I went over it, I caught air and saw another weirdly shaped mogul that I had not seen earlier. "That is not good," I thought, and as soon as I landed, I fell and heard this "beep" sound. Immediately, I knew something was wrong. I had been snowboarding in Colorado for eight years and had never heard such a sinister sound in my life.

"It's going to be okay. It's going to be okay," I kept telling myself as I lay on the snow. After few deep breaths, I tried to get up, but something was different. I tried again, but something was wrong. I could not move my body. It was a strange experience. I tried again . . . and again . . . and again. Nothing happened. I soon saw Sean falling about five feet away from me. "I can't move my body. I can't move my body," I mumbled. I wanted to shout for help but could barely speak. He could not understand what I was saying at first.

"I cannot hear you. What are you saying?"

"I cannot move my body."

"Don't joke about that kind of stuff."

"I am serious. Call 9–1–1. 9–1–1."

Finally he understood that something was terribly wrong but he was hesitant to leave me. I told him that it was the best option, and finally, with fear and anxiety, he went down to get help. As the sound of his snowboard gliding away faded, I was all alone on the mountain. The sky was still as blue as the ocean, but darkness was descending on my mind. I thought that perhaps if I tried to move again in a few minutes, my hands and legs would move again. Taking a deep breath, slowly and religiously, I tried to move them, but nothing happened. "Shit. Something is definitely wrong." I tried to move different parts of my body. I could barely turn my head and move my shoulders on both sides. While I was checking my condition, I suddenly felt my whole body sliding down the mountain. I could not stop myself and could not do anything about it. I had to let my body slide down the steep trail. Slowly, after few seconds, I stopped sliding.

It was silent. I could feel nothing but my fear and frustration. I did not want to think about anything at the moment, knowing that this was a serious situation and fearing that actually thinking about it would confirm that and intensify my fear and frustration. About five minutes later I heard the sound of people snowboarding and talking. "Help!" I cried, trying to get their attention, but my desperate effort failed. Fortunately, they saw me laying on the snow and came closer to me to check on me. I was grateful that they had stopped to help. Someone asked if I was okay, and I said no, I needed help. "9–1–1, 9–1–1," I said. They told me they would get help and asked if I would be okay by myself. I wanted one of them to stay with me but could not think clearly enough to ask. So I said yes and thanked them.

Again, I was left alone. I did not want to pray to God because a prayer would affirm my dire situation, but at the same time I was afraid to let go of God, so I slowly recited the Lord's Prayer while waiting for the ski patrol: "Our Father in heaven. Your kingdom come. Our Father lead us not into temptation. Deliver us. Our Father. . . . Your will be done on earth as it is in heaven. . . . For yours is the kingdom and the power and the glory forever, Amen." The words of the prayer were all mixed up, but that did not matter. God was the only audience of my prayer, and as long as he could hear me saying these mixed words of prayer, I was okay. It was better than doing nothing.

Finally, ski patrol agents came up and asked me a few questions regarding my condition and memory. They removed my bag, snowboard, gloves, goggles, and beanie, then they cut through my thick ski jackets and shirts and put a medical collar on my neck. "We are going to transfer you to this sled on three. One, two, three." They transferred me to the sled that was attached to the snowmobile. Since I was still near the top of the mountain, it took a long time to get down and to go around moguls. It was a bumpy ride. I had always wanted to ride a snowmobile, but not like this.

When the ride was over, an ambulance was waiting for us to transfer me to a hospital in Aspen. There Sean looked at me anxiously, wanting to encourage me but not knowing what to say. Before I left, I told him that I would be okay. I asked him not to call my parents but to give my friend Gary's information to the hospital so that I could use the health insurance registered under his name.

The medical team was waiting for us near the entrance of the hospital in Aspen and transferred me to a small room to run a few examinations. I do not remember clearly what happened next. What I do remember is that after a few examinations, they put me on a helicopter to transfer me to St. Mary's Hospital in Grand Junction instead of to a hospital in Denver because the weather conditions were too severe to fly me to Denver. It was my first time riding a helicopter, but again, there was no excitement, only the desperate sound of my voice reciting the prayer, "Our Father in heaven .

.. Amen." As soon as the helicopter landed at the hospital, the medical team rushed me into the operating room. A surgeon put a mask on my face for anesthesia. It was my first time undergoing surgery, so out of fear of waking up in the middle of it, I took a deep breath as if smoking a cigarette. I hoped that the procedure would fix whatever was going on with my body and return everything to normal.

Around 4:00 p.m. on the day of my accident, Dad received a strange call from the hospital in Aspen. He could not quite understand the message, but it seemed to be that his son—with whom he had talked just a few hours earlier—was in critical condition and in need of urgent surgery. After that call, he received another one from Sean which cleared up part of the confusion. After I was put in the ambulance, Sean followed it and registered my information at the hospital in Aspen as I had directed. He was as worried as I was and asked the medical teams about my condition. They did not give him a clear answer but hinted that it was serious. He then decided to call Dad and told him that I would be transferred to the hospital in Grand Junction, Colorado.

After the two calls, Dad asked Mr. Lee, one of the deacons of his church, to drive with him to the hospital. When they arrived, I was still in surgery. The surgeon came out and explained to him that the surgery "went well." Without understanding the nature of the injury, the doctor's words sounded reassuring. After seeing me awake, Mr. Lee drove back to Denver and Sean drove to Aspen, while Dad stayed with me at the hospital. It was only much later that I understood what had happened during surgery. The surgeon performed spinal fusion surgery to connect the C-3, C-4, and C-5 vertebrae because my C-4 and C-5 were broken. They were screwed with bolts and held together by a metal plate. However, I did not understand the consequence of this procedure.

St. Mary's Hospital

On December 14, 2004, when I opened my eyes and found myself in a hospital bed in the Intensive Care Unit (ICU) with many IV lines in my arms and a monitor showing my vitals next to my bed, I slowly tried to figure out what was happening. I remembered the dream I'd had of snowboarding with my friends, falling and not being able to move, and riding on a snowmobile. I was actually somewhat relieved by the thought that I was still dreaming, for all I would have to do would be to wake up from the nightmare. But the intense pain in my shoulders and body when I tried to move my fingers and toes told me that I was not dreaming anymore. "Crap, it was not a dream." I turned my head to one side, and seeing Dad sleeping next to me in a chair in an uncomfortable position calmed me down. I fell back asleep.

For about the fifth time, I saw two ghostly figures sitting at the end of my hospital bed. They talked to each other excitedly but never engaged in any conversation with me. Was I overdosing on pain killers and hallucinating? Was I dreaming again? If they were actual people, they would have talked to me. No, they were real and there in my dark hospital room. I believed they were ghosts. I was afraid of making eye contact with them as it seemed scary. As I saw them more often, I did not feel any sense of fear anymore. However, I had nightmares that recurred, and one particular nightmare of seeing myself falling down and being sucked into this deep dark void of nothingness again and again was terrifying. I woke up from the nightmares screaming and gasping for breath. Were the images in the nightmares prophetic visions of my future? Was I trapped in the deep, dark hole?

I believe it was a few days later that the general managers from Matsuhisa, Aku *san*, Sean, and Asa visited me. They told me how sorry they were, and I was relieved when they assured me that the restaurant's insurance had great medical and financial benefits. They expressed concern that I could not work during that season. Many of my co-workers had written encouraging messages on a card, and Sako *san* sent a sushi and sashimi platter, which Dad enjoyed very much since I had no appetite at all. As they were leaving the hospital, they said, "Everything is going to be okay. Don't worry." I smiled, but could not appreciate their visit nor the effort they made to drive to Grand Junction from Aspen. Neither was I able to express my gratitude to the medical team at St. Mary's Hospital who took very good care of me. I was probably very rude and resistant to their efforts to help me. I do not remember much about my hospitalization at St. Mary's Hospital beyond these memories.

During my nine days of hospitalization I lay in the hospital bed all day, not knowing what was going on. Perhaps the doctors and nurses explained to me about the nature, purpose, and result of the surgery and possible consequences of the injury, but all I heard was "blah, blah, blah." Maybe pain medication numbed my ability to understand their medical explanations, for wasn't I curious to know the condition of my body and to know why the surgery did not fix my hands and feet? Perhaps fear of learning the answers and understanding my new reality paralyzed my mind. The possibility of paralysis might have crossed my mind or was mentioned by the medical team, but I could not comprehend it. Whatever was going on in my mind, the time in the hospital room passed rapidly. Dad stayed by my side except when he left to lead the worship service back in Denver the following Sunday. On the ninth day of my hospitalization, I was put on a private plane to Denver to be transferred to Craig Hospital, a non-profit rehabilitation hospital for people with spinal cord and traumatic brain injuries located in Englewood, Colorado. I was hopeful of being fixed and of things returning to normal.

Part 3

My Life at Craig Hospital

I was uncertain of the level of my injury but I knew I just needed time to rest, heal, and rehabilitate my body. After all, that is why I was transferred to Craig Hospital, where I would get the highest quality of medical treatment and therapy. My parents were praying for a full recovery. God would answer the prayers of such faithful believers. I knew that I would walk out of the hospital in a few months. I would be back to work soon enough and would resume my goal of becoming a successful sushi chef and business owner. Pursuing my dreams had been interrupted, but only momentarily. It was just a matter of time before I would be back on my feet.

Craig Hospital

After I was admitted to Craig Hospital, things moved fast. Nurses pushed my bed, parked it in the examining room, got rid of the IV lines, and left the room. Soon, two therapists entered the room and began an assessment to determine the level of my injury. The assessment included hundreds of questions that assessed whether I could move my thumb, pinky, or any fingers. Could I move my ankle, leg, toe, or shoulder? Could I touch my hands without moving my shoulders? When I thought it was over, one of them pulled a needle out of her bag and told me that she would poke different parts of my body. She then poked me, smiling, and repeatedly asked, "Can you feel this?" Sometimes I could, but I could not always distinguish whether I felt pressure or actual pain. And when I thought a poke was painful, I could not always tell if it was dull, mild, or sharp. The nurse probably explained to me why they were torturing me with their needles, but I could not understand.

The result of the assessment was that I had a spinal cord injury (SCI) at the C-4 and C-5 vertebrae, and that level of injury meant that I was paralyzed from my shoulders down, although this understanding only became clear much later on. I could move my shoulders and wrists, but without my triceps functioning, I could not move my fingers. People who had lower injury levels often used manual wheelchairs. The level of my injury was "B incomplete," with "B" indicating the level of my physical movement, and "incomplete" indicating a partial ability to feel certain parts of my body. I had sensation in certain parts of my body, but not like before. In other areas I either had no sensation at all or they felt differently, so that instead of sharp pain, I would feel pressure or dull pain. If I had had no sensation at all, my injury level would have been "B complete." The nurses added that it was very important for me to know the details of my injury so that I could avoid certain activities and would know to report it if I ever felt something odd or different, as well as explain my situation to others in the case of emergency.

In order to prepare a customized electric wheelchair that would perfectly fit my body, detailed measurements were taken of my height and weight and the length of arms and legs right after the assessment. Customized wheelchairs help prevent tremendous pain and extreme discomfort in people with spinal cord injuries who lack the ability to adjust their posture. After the assessment and measurements were taken, the physical therapy team assembled a used electric wheelchair for me until they could order a new one, which cost about $20,000.

Craig Hospital felt like a different country. The doctors, nurses, and clinal nurse assistants—referred to as "techs"—used many medical words that I did not understand. I knew that they were trying to help me, but I could not understand them. I did not even understand the level of my injury and the reason why I was there. My broken English might have been the cause of my misunderstandings, but I was too stubborn to acknowledge this obstacle and ask for a Korean interpreter. Was I trying to preserve my pride? If so, was it worth it?

I might have been ignorant of the situation because I was convinced that I would walk out of the hospital within three months. No doctor, nurse, or psychologist ever mentioned anything about three months, but that is what I thought. Was it because Dad's pastor friends came to my hospital room and prayed for me? Could it have been because of Dad's encouragement? He often told me not to worry about my injury because God would heal me. Could it have been my past experiences of participating in church activities? It could have been my faith in my parents' faith since I observed them to be sincere Christians. Surely God would hear their prayers even if he might not hear mine. I believed so strongly that I would walk out of Craig that when an Asian social worker offered to help me, I gently and faithfully told him that God would heal me and refused it. Maybe I misunderstood the doctor when he told me that I could be *discharged* after two or three months. Wherever the source of my faith, I was certain that I would walk again and be back to normal soon.

Daily Life

Life at Craig Hospital was busy. I was teamed with a physical therapist, occupational therapist, social worker, psychologist, doctor, and several techs, and they gave me a very busy and tough schedule during the weekdays. Just like them, I had weekends off. Physical and occupational sessions were usually held in the morning and afternoon in a big recreational room. I was paired with at least one physical or occupational therapist who stayed next to me. The room was packed with people and full of energy and passion. Everyone seemed to be working hard, especially the therapists and techs. My occupational therapist, Shonna, had me attempt ordinary, daily tasks such as using a computer mouse, typing, lifting forks and spoons, brushing my teeth, grasping objects without using my fingers, opening doors, pushing buttons in the elevator, and so forth. She took me outside to drive my wheelchair around the hospital and go over unpaved roads, dirt, and grass so that I could learn to maneuver my wheelchair. She gave me two helpful pieces of equipment that I could use for different tasks: plastic typing sticks and universal cuffs. The typing sticks allowed me to type words on the keyboard. The cuffs, when put on my hands like a bracelet, allowed me to put an object into a hole so that I could use the object for different tasks.

For physical therapy sessions, there were times when patients exercised or stretched in their wheelchairs. These exercises were very basic and simple and would not appear to be real exercises for people without SCI, but for someone like me who could not even lift a fork to poke at food and bring it to my mouth, lifting my arms once or twice was challenging. The hospital was fully equipped for rehabilitation with a gym and swimming pool for therapeutic use. I tried swimming therapy twice, and it was a great experience. But my favorite place was an outside resting area right in front of the gym. There was a small table and three chairs for people to take a break, but no one seemed to use it during the wintertime. I stayed out there about an hour every day, tilting my wheelchair (to prevent pressure sores), staring at the blue sky, and enjoying the silence. I did not regret past actions or worry about the future; I did not think about anything. The cold fresh air strangely refreshed me. Maybe I felt trapped and suffocated in the hospital or was tired of focusing on the reality that I had been unable to accept as mine. For whatever reason, it felt nice out there. I wore only a fleece and a pair of sweatpants as I had not yet recognized that my sensation of cold was temporarily lost due to the injury.

I See Stars

One day my physical therapist, Carey, recommended that I use exercise equipment which helps patients stand up straight. I was excited but also reluctant because I thought, "I will eventually stand and walk out of this hospital, so what is the point of this exercise? Oh well, I will give it a shot as a practice to walk out of here." She and the techs transferred me to the machine and put a belt around my chest. Slowly, I was standing up just like I was able to do few weeks prior and was very happy and excited for a short moment, thinking that I would be standing in three months. But I quickly felt very dizzy and told them about seeing many small stars. They quickly held my head and body and transferred me to my wheelchair and then to the therapy table. As soon as they put me on the table, I felt more light-headedness, saw more stars, and passed out. Hearing some sort of sound woke me up, and it was Carey calling my name "Gary, are you okay? Wake up!" (People at Craig called me Gary at first because I was still using his information for insurance).

While it felt as if I was out for an hour or more, I was told it was only a minute or so. I lay on the therapy table for some time. When I came to my senses, I could hear other therapists and patients talking about me, "He totally passed out. He was gone for few minutes." Blackouts caused by low blood pressure were normal occurrences for certain patients in the gym, but they were still notable events. After experiencing what it was like to pass out, I learned its precursors—feeling drowsiness and dizziness and seeing stars—and ways to prevent them from causing blackouts such as reclining my wheelchair, taking deep breaths, getting fresh air, and putting myself in a safe position just in case I blacked out to avoid losing control of my wheelchair.

The Most Humiliating Day

I still remember the most humiliating day of my life. I had never felt so ashamed before. Not long after my first blackout, I was on the therapy table participating in the group therapy exercise. Afterward, I laid on the table for about thirty minutes and was ready to get back on my wheelchair. As Carey tried to pull me up by pulling my hands, I felt something on my stomach and thought, "No, this is not what I think is going to happen." But yes, a twenty-two-year-old old man just pooped in his pants in the middle of a room filled with people. Carey and a tech asked me quietly if something happened, and I nodded. They quickly responded to my accident. Unfortunately there was no way to manage the accident privately. They brought bed pads and put them on my wheelchair; they transferred me to my wheelchair and wiped the table with sanitizer. Everyone knew what had happened. Trying my best to avoid eye contact, I focused on driving my wheelchair to my room as quickly as possible.

Carey told me not to worry about it because I did not have control over my body. She tried to assure me that it happened all the time. But after the tech finished cleaning up after me and left the room, tears fell for a few minutes. Humiliation and embarrassment pierced my heart and caused so much pain. "Is this my future? Am I a baby that now someone must help me to take a shit and clean after me? I cannot live like this. This is not life. This is a curse, some dark, evil shit and destruction." I could not digest the bitter reality of what happened for some time, especially in an environment where I had to act like I was okay enough to start another round of rehab. I kept motivating myself, "Let's wait for just two months. Then everything will be okay. I will walk again. I will have control over my bowels soon. This is *only* temporary." And I moved on and exercised as hard as I could, as if nothing happened, disguising the truth.

Seeing a Familiar Stranger

One time, all of a sudden, my body began shaking uncontrollably. It was the first time my body moved at all since the accident. "Yes! My body is finally becoming normal," I thought. But the shaking continued involuntarily. I was not doing it and was not controlling it. Carey asked me if I was causing the movements and I told her, "I wish." She smiled and explained that such involuntary movements are called spasms, which are normal for people with spinal cord injuries, and that the cause is unknown. She said I needed to start taking medication for body and bladder spasms, and that I needed guard rails on my bed and straps on my feet to prevent them from dancing around without control. I really did not like her suggestions and I wondered what possible harm the spasms could cause me. So I decided to wait for a few days. Three nights later I found my whole body shaking uncontrollably and I almost fell off the bed. And then the next morning, when I was in wheelchair, my feet started moving randomly all over the place. At that point I understood that Carey was not trying to scare me. Dan, who helped me with wheelchair and equipment-related issues, brought straps and installed them on the footplates of my wheelchair. Two black straps now covered both of my feet and confined them to the footplates. The black straps were signs that my feet no longer functioned as they were created to do.

    I had avoided looking at myself in a mirror for almost two weeks. Had I noticed or understood the changes that had already occurred to me after the snowboarding accident? There were half-height mirrors in the elevators at Craig Hospital to help patients maneuver their wheelchairs. When I saw myself in the mirrors, I would quickly look elsewhere. But when I finally looked, I was surprised to see a familiar stranger. I was about thirty pounds lighter and my face was thinner, my hair longer, and I was in a wheelchair. However, this version no longer moved his arms like me, walked like me, smiled like me, looked like me, or felt like me. He did not even have enough arm strength to hold a fork and bring bread to his mouth. He could not use the toilet by himself and was so embarrassed he wept quietly. He would go outside to get some fresh air only to forget that he could no longer open a closed door by himself and would have to wait for someone to open the door for him. I did not want him. I did not like him. I denied him, rejected him, hated him, and even cursed him. I should not be him. I could not be him. I must not be him. Was I supposed to accept this version as myself? Would rejecting it be too cruel? What would happen if I did? Accepting him was like accepting a stranger that I did not invite to my house.

From Walking to Wheeling

My Name Is Not Gary

After about a month passed by, I received a call from my friend Gary, whose information I had used to work at Matsuhisa and whose insurance I was using after my accident. He asked me how I was doing and I told him that I felt like shit. But he was not calling just to check on me. He told me that he was in trouble; his parents found out about me using his information because they had received my medical bills. They were really upset and frustrated and he said I needed to do something. I told him I needed to think about it. At first I was mad at him. What did he expect me to do? I was all messed up and confined to a wheelchair, and he was telling me to do something when I could not do anything.

I did not know anything about health insurance, Medicaid, and hospital bills. Nor did I know that using an ambulance and staying at an ICU was costly. I did not know that the government could help American citizens and permanent residents with disabilities with medical bills, living expenses, scholarships, and so forth. I did not know that using my friend's information and receiving benefits from his health insurance and the government could cause serious problems for him. In fact, I thought using insurance was like using a credit card. I would use a portion of his health insurance and government benefits and then pay them back later. I thought that the total medical bill would be less than $30,000 and that I would move my body within three months and return to work in a year or so and pay them back.

The hospitals in Aspen and Grand Junction had already submitted their claims to insurance and to government agencies, and Craig Hospital was taking the same path. Thus people at St. Mary's Hospital and Craig knew me as Gary. Fortunately my parents understood the urgency of the situation and contacted Sandy, a Korean lawyer's assistant. She contacted the hospitals and was able to explain the situation to Lucy my Clinical Care Manager, at Craig Hospital, and my name was finally corrected. While Sandy was working with them, my parents met Gary's parents and apologized on my behalf and promised that they would take care of the issue. I am thankful that they forgave my mistakes. Unfortunately, because of my ego and ambition, I lost contact with Gary.

Having to adjust all the files to my correct name caused extra work for social workers and the medical record team at Craig. But now there was also the huge issue of taking care of the medical expenses. Without legal immigration status, they could offer no further help. The order for a new wheelchair was canceled; all the medical charges and other expenses that had been billed to Gary's insurance company and government agencies had to be rescinded; and the orders for other medical and therapeutic equipment, supplies, and items were canceled. Medical bills from the hospitals in Aspen and Grand Junction were on their way to my house, but I did not know that at that time.

Visits from My Friends

During my stay I had many visitors and it was good to see my friends. They brought balloons, cards, and food and were somewhat shocked to see me in an electric wheelchair with paralysis. They were frustrated for me and at a loss for words. Still, they were courageous. Their messages (such as "Hope you get better soon!," "Praying for your healing," and "Let's party when you get out") were positive and encouraging. I was happy to finally see my friend Josh because all I had been thinking about for the last two or three weeks was wanting to smoke a cigarette. As soon as I saw him, we went outside to smoke. He asked me if it was okay for me to smoke, and I told him, "Hell yeah." He handed me a cigarette, but I could not even hold it. So I had him put it on my mouth and light it. I took a deep drag, but as soon as I did, I began coughing like it was my first time smoking and I spit it out. I coughed so badly that he was hesitant to put the cigarette in my mouth again. This time I did not inhale deeply, but I still coughed. For some reason, I did not enjoy the experience like I used to. But I was happy to at least have gotten the taste and smell of a cigarette. I later learned that the coughing was caused by my body's inability to get the smoke out of my lungs completely.

My co-workers and the executive chef from Aspen drove to Denver to see me. He told me that when I could move again, I could work with him again. That was a great motivator. A few days later, an ex-girlfriend visited me and gave me a card. The card was about me getting well and her wanting to get back together, but I did not hear from her after that visit. A few friends from high school came and hung with me for some time. One friend dropped off Korean comedy programs, and there were a few times that I laughed so hard that tears came out, which was odd because I had never laughed like that before. I later found out that I was on Prozac. I did not know what it was but it helped me endure the time in the hospital. Laughter was good medicine, but Prozac was better. My friend James, who was living in Las Vegas, came to see me after hearing about the accident. Naturally I took him outside to smoke. He also seemed concerned about handing me a cigarette, but I encouraged him that it would be fine. Once again, the usually sweet taste of the cigarette was just bitter and distasteful.

I figured my friends could not possibly understand what I was going through. If I had been honest with them, every time they asked me how I felt, I should have said that I was lonely, sad, depressed, angry, suicidal, and hopeless. I felt these emotions throughout every day. Sure, my friends might feel sympathy but would not be able to handle all my negativities. So what would be the point of sharing my true feelings to my loved ones who were already suffering in their own context and of inflicting discomfort upon them just so that I could feel better and get things off my chest? Was I undermining their ability and capacity to help me psychologically? I did not want to add more baggage or burden to my loved ones. So I determined to avoid talking about my feelings and just suck it up.

Sean Is Coming to Town

About six weeks later, I received a call from Sean. He'd had a snowboarding accident and was hospitalized in Aspen, Colorado. His right elbow and right hip bone were broken so severely that he needed surgery to put bolts in his elbow. He called me as he was about to be transferred from a hospital in Aspen to a hospital in Denver for the surgery. He asked me the name of my hospital and Sean realized that Swedish Hospital, where he was headed, was next to Craig.

At first I was furious that he was so negligent and careless as to get into an accident. "Did he not just see his friend who broke his neck and is in a wheelchair? Not even a month has passed since my accident—how could he go snowboarding so soon?" After my anger and frustration subsided, excitement soon filled my heart at the thought of seeing my friend in this lonely place. A few days later, Sean called me after the surgery. It had gone well, but he would need a few months of rehabilitation to regain strength in his elbow and hip. Before rehab, he would need to remain hospitalized while he gained strength. He would be stuck at Swedish for a few weeks.

After rehabilitation one morning, I took the elevator to the basement of Craig Hospital. There was a basement hallway which connected Craig Hospital to Swedish Hospital, which allowed patients to be transferred between the two hospitals. This was my first time wheeling down the hallway to the hospital, but it was not difficult to find his room because I was treated like a VIP because of my electric wheelchair. When I asked for directions, staff at Swedish Hospital kindly helped me and even showed me the way. When I finally found the room and saw Sean in a hospital gown, I laughed at him and said, "What happened to you brother? Didn't you see what happened to me? You careless man." He laughed too. We never thought that we would meet under such circumstances.

At first he had to use a manual wheelchair because he did not have the arm strength to use a walker or cane. Using the wheelchair was difficult for him because he could only use his left arm to maneuver his wheelchair. When he pushed his chair with his left arm, he could only go in circles. When he showed me, we both laughed for a long time. Sean was sharing the room with another patient, so we tried to figure out a way to get out of his room and back to mine, which was bigger and had more things to do. Since he needed someone to either push his wheelchair from behind or pull him from the front, we had to experiment.

After a few trials, I had him grasp the back of my wheelchair so I could pull him. It worked, but the problem was that his arm was not quite long enough. So he found a thin bed sheet, tied it on the back of my chair, and took hold of that. Having only 1.5 horsepower on my electric wheelchair, we moved slowly, but adrenaline filled us completely. I had to be careful lest I stop too abruptly and cause his wheelchair to hit the backside of my chair, which would make him scream in pain, both jokingly and seriously. As we wheeled to Craig Hospital, we caught the attention of all the people who saw us. They responded with smiles and shouts such as, "Way to go! That is awesome!"

During the two or three weeks of his hospitalization, we hung out every day just like before. I showed him my favorite spots around Craig Hospital. We watched Korean television programs. We would talk about our past, but not about anything related to my condition because I did not want to and because I was confident that I would be walking out of the hospital that there was no need to talk about it. When I was with him, I was free to talk about my glorious past. One time Sean said, "I think the reason I am at Swedish is to be with you." "No, it was your careless snowboarding style!" I responded, and we both laughed. Was he right? Did God send him to be with me? But if so, if I will walk out of here in three months, why is he here?

Picnic at Craig

During the whole stay at Craig, I had no appetite. It might have been due to the horrible food at Craig. Maybe I was being too picky because other patients at Craig seemed to eat the hospital food without complaining. Maybe I felt too depressed or just did not feel like eating. Doctors were worried that losing weight could slow down my rehabilitation process. Dad graciously brought me Korean food. One time he actually brought a portable mini stove with him so that we could have a Korean BBQ party. He had even brought kimchi. I told him that the smell would fill the room and the whole hospital! But he said not to worry; we would do it outside. He set it up at my favorite spot. Because it was still winter, no one else was there. He brought everything needed. With that set up, it was like we were dining in a Korean restaurant. It was the best Korean BBQ I had ever had in my entire life. Dad grilled the meat and fed it to me because I lacked the strength to lift a fork. I was overwhelmed with a strange mixture of gratitude and sorrow.

The Hardest Thing I Have Ever Had to Say

My faith in my ability to walk out of the hospital faced a breaking point. Slowly I began to analyze my mysterious confidence and began wondering if I actually would walk again. I considered two reasonable and related questions. The first question was, "Should I not at least be able to move a finger or two if I am going to walk out of here?" It had been almost two months since the accident and I still had no new movements. I tried very hard to move my body until I felt dizzy during physical therapy sessions and Carey told me to stop. I tried to imagine myself moving around, hoping a mind control practice could help my body awaken from its sleep.

The second question was, "Why am I receiving training and lectures to prepare me for living with a disability?" When I began rehab at Craig Hospital, I simply followed the instructions of my therapists thinking that they were helping me to move again. But as time passed by and as my body was still as stiff as a log, I began to realize that they were helping me learn to live with paralysis in a wheelchair. Craig Hospital was not a place that repaired disabilities and resuscitated dead spinal cord nerves. That was why patients did rehab, went in groups to public places in their wheelchairs, joined classes to learn how to use different modes of transportation, and learned how to take care of their bodies. At that point I finally knew something was terribly wrong and that I needed a clear understanding of my injury and reality. So I invited my primary doctor to tell me the truth.

Dad and I met with my primary doctor and asked him why progress was so slow in regaining body movements. He paused for a moment and then explained to me that the spinal cord is like a wire that connects my brain to different parts of my body. To move my legs, my brain sends a signal, the signal is transferred through my spinal cord nerves to my legs, and then they move. But now when my brain sent a signal, it couldn't be delivered through my spinal cord because it was injured at the C-5 vertebra (the area of my shoulders). That was why I could move the parts of my body that were above the injury level but not the parts of my body that were below it. He went on to explain that my brain is like an internet company, my body is like a computer, and my spinal cord is like the wire. Everything works great except that the wire is disconnected.

I wanted to know more. I asked how he could repair the broken nerves. He explained that stem cells could regenerate the broken nerves of the spinal cord injury, and with optimism and laughter, I told him, "All right, I am ready for the stem cell therapy or surgery, whatever you doctors call it. Give me some stem cells!" But the technology did not yet exist and the doctor was not sure when a treatment would be developed for spinal cord injuries. Frustrated, I asked when I could walk again without the treatment and what the percentage was of me walking again. He answered, "I could be wrong, but you may not walk for the rest of your life. I'm sorry." I could only thank him for his honest answer.

Gravity and silence filled the room after his departure. My heart was filled with sorrow, disappointment, and pain. My eyes nearly filled with tears. I felt a touch on my shoulder and was about to burst into tears. I turned towards Dad to explain the doctor's answer to him but stopped when I saw an unexpected and almost innocent, childlike smile on his face. "Wow! He is ninety-nine percent sure that you can walk again, right?" English is not our first language, but how could he get it so wrong? I wasn't sure if he was giving me a spiritual and divine interpretation of the death sentence decreed by the doctor or a faith-filled answer dependent on God.

I could not ruin his joy at that moment. I could hardly respond to him but holding back tears, I told him, "Yes, the doctor was certain that I could walk again. I am going to get some fresh air." Then I went to my hiding place and cried my heart out. My nerves received a death sentence. The next day, I told Dad exactly what the doctor said in the room. He, who was not easily shaken emotionally, denied the report at first but soon broke down in tears. I found out that he had already shared the false report with Mom. We were too afraid to tell her the truth at that time because she was so excited that I would walk again. Dad told me that he would take care of this issue.

Death Sentence

I was completely broken in every way. My confidence and hope of walking out of Craig in three months were shattered into a million pieces without any possibility of repair. I was finally awake from my fantasy and faced the cruel reality for the first time since the accident. I thought I was dreaming a nightmare, but the reality was worse. I could not believe that it actually happened to me. I knew I was not a saint. I used drugs, drank alcohol, and was engaged in activities that could be defined as "worldly things" according to the standard of the Bible. But they did not harm anybody. I had simply followed the path of making myself "happy" according to the world's standards, although they did not make my parents happy. The price of my accident was too heavy. It was not fair. I thought this type of tragedy only happened in movies and dramas. I never thought that it could happen to me.

Out of fear and anxiety, I cautiously began imagining the very near future of my life. But the future seemed too dark to see, too complicated to simplify, too bitter to swallow, too uncertain to accept, and too much to bear by myself. As anxiety colored my views and fear became the music to my ears, "failure" became the world to me. I failed. I failed to accomplish my dreams. I failed my parents who loved me as I was and who were patient with me during my rebellious teenage and young adult years. I failed my friends who trusted me. I failed myself. I wondered what there was to do if I could not walk for the rest of my life. What was the point of having a big house if I couldn't even go to the basement and second floor? What was the point of a fancy car if I couldn't drive it? What was the meaning of life if I couldn't move my arms and legs? I could not even shower or shit by myself.

Thoughts of Suicide

I became so depressed that I began telling myself that my life was over. I wondered what I could do for the rest of my life. Who was going to like me?

I told myself that no one liked me. No one wanted me. I was just a burden on society and to my friends and parents. Without legal status, how was I going to support myself financially? My friends could not help me. My parents might take care of me for a while, but what would happen when they became tired of it? What if they kicked me out or got divorced? I would be so miserable and humiliated. I thought that I should just take my life right then and spare myself from pain and humiliation and keep my dignity and pride. My parents and friends would be sad for some time but would move on. Indeed, they would not have to suffer to take care of me. They would be free from the shackles of their parenting responsibilities and be free to live their lives fully without the stress of taking care of me and worrying about my future. I thought it would be the least and best I could do for them. And maybe that was what they wanted anyway. Was it the devil whispering lies or truths to me, or was my mind just going crazy from depression, fear, and negative thoughts?

I thought about a few options, but when I saw the emergency stairs sign, I thought that falling down the stairwell in the three-hundred-pound wheelchair would surely do the job. I just needed to find the appropriate time to do it. Was I serious about the decision? Was I not afraid of death or hell? Perhaps I thought that going to hell was better than living in this world with a disability and going through various hardships. Maybe I did not think much at all about the afterlife. What was certain was that in the process of thinking about heading towards the stairway, other thoughts and memories interrupted the process.

Slowly I remembered the stories of the Bible that I learned from attending Sunday school and from listening to boring sermons preached by many pastors, including Dad. Did I really believe the stories? Did I believe in God? At the very least I did not deny the existence of God, nor the stories that were recorded in the Bible including the miracles that happened during the times of the Old Testament and New Testament. However, there was never a time when I seriously thought about my beliefs about God, although there were a few times when I prayed to God for various reasons. The most important thing was that I reached out to God and prayed to him: "Lord," I prayed, "I am not sure if I truly believe the narratives that are stated in the Bible. Yes, I went to church when I was a child, participated in various church activities, and learned many things about you and the Bible. Honestly, I am not sure if I really believe you or not. But if you can still do something about my life, and can still heal me as the Bible states, and if it is not too late, please heal me and hold my hands. In Jesus's name, Amen."

I opened my eyes and tried to move my arms and legs, but nothing happened. I laughed, but it was not a laughter of doubt. Instead, I wanted to try God out (that is how I felt at the moment). I wanted to really explore this faith to figure out why my parents devoted their lives to it and, most importantly, whether it could really heal me or not. I was serious this time and decided that I would do my best and give my best to this religion so that I would not have any regrets when it failed me. I had nothing to lose. If I could walk again that would be great; but if I could not, that would prove that religion was not worth pursuing and help me to make a logical and reasonable decision. I was not going anywhere so taking my life could wait at least for a year. I thought that a year could be enough to test the religion.

CICP Card

About two weeks before the discharge date, Lucy encouraged me to apply for a Colorado Indigents Care Program (CICP) card because I had no medical insurance or assistance. She told me that I could receive some medical support through the program. I did not feel like going anywhere, especially on that day. It was cloudy and gloomy but Dad insisted that we should check it out. Driving to the office to apply for a card was a lot of work. Not having a modified van, it was somewhat tricky to be transferred from a wheelchair to the sedan, though Carey had trained us. Dad opened the passenger door, and I parked myself close to the passenger seat. After disassembling the ledge and armrest of the left side of my wheelchair, he put a sliding board under my hip and slid me from my wheelchair to the seat of the car. He had to work in a tight and small space between the car and my wheelchair and put the manual wheelchair in the backseat. We wrestled with the transfer for thirty minutes or so. But once we got to the office, it did not take a long time to apply and be approved because recipients simply had to be residents of Colorado in financial need; I was the perfect candidate. We did not expect too much from the program but thought it would be better than nothing. We were half right and half wrong.

Hospital Bills from Craig Hospital

After I told Lucy about my undocumented immigration status, my family soon realized that I had to pay for the hospital bills. It was nearing time for me to be discharged from the hospital and pay the bills. On the last day at Craig, I asked Lucy about the medical bills, and she told me that the hospital decided to cancel the medical bills, understanding that my family was in great financial need and could not afford to pay them, even if they would eventually be transferred to collection agencies.

My family had prayed about this problem and had made some calculations to figure out the cost of the bills. I had many techs who helped me every day for sixty days or more; I was treated by nurses on a daily basis and seen by doctors and social workers; I received various rehab equipment, medical supplies, and physical and occupational therapies; and I stayed at Craig's state-of-the-art facility with a private, spacious room for two and a half months. But we had no idea what the cost of medical care would be. She did not tell me the exact amount of the total bill but mentioned that it was above $100,000. (About ten years after the discharge, I asked her about the cost of the bills, and she answered that it could have been up to $250,000). Prayer moved the minds of the leadership of the hospital.

Discharge Day

On discharge day I had been at Craig Hospital for almost two and a half months. I had to have a final discharge meeting with my parents, Lucy a doctor, plus two more hospital employees. Sandy was on the speaker phone to translate for my parents. Toward the end of the meeting, one of the Craig team members asked my parents whether they understood the nature of my spinal cord injury and the possibility that I may never walk again. When it was Sandy's turn to translate the grave question for my parents, she hesitated for a moment before slowly translating it in Korean. As she was asking the question in Korean, I just looked down and sighed.

"What is going on?" Mom asked us. "I thought you could walk again." No one said anything. She looked at each of us with a confused look and asked Dad one more time, "What is going on? You told me that the primary doctor said that our son can walk again." Tears were streaming down her face. Dad handed her tissues and tried to comfort her, but she shook her head and turned away from him. She asked Sandy to tell her the truth.

One of the team members articulated my condition very clearly: "The possibility of him walking again is very low. We are terribly sorry about this. We thought that you already knew about this." After hearing Sandy's crystal-clear translation, Mom stood up and walked out of the room. Dad wanted her to stay in the room until the meeting was over, but she resisted him and said that she had heard enough. After the meeting, for a few days Mom did not eat or work and she cried all day and night.

The long but short time at Craig Hospital was finally over. After treating me for three months and canceling my medical bills, they gave me the electric wheelchair that I had been using in the hospital, a manual wheelchair, a lift machine that transfers a patient from a wheelchair to bed, a shower chair, and other items and supplies to assist with my daily needs. Unfortunately I could not share my gratitude with the people who helped me. I honestly could not think about anything or anyone else except myself at that moment. It was somewhat scary leaving the hospital knowing that I would not have the same accommodating environment and support outside of Craig. However, I was excited to be out of the hospital setting. I hoped that I would not have to come back here, at least not in my wheelchair.

Part 4

Broken Life

Our lives were in upheaval. My parents' only child had a life-changing accident and would probably never walk again. Because of this, their lives changed significantly as well. Visits to the hospital continued as I encountered complications. Bills we could not pay were mounting. Dad received little encouragement or support from his church, which was going through a significant transition as he was caring for me. Mom was the sole earner in the family and increasingly regretted our family ever moving to the US. My parents could not relieve my pain and suffering, and despite their prayers, it did not seem like God was going to either; their faith was in crisis. Meanwhile, I found myself reaching out to God in prayer more and more and also cursing both the day that I was born and the day I had gone snowboarding with my friends.

New Home!

In anticipation of my discharge, Dad had been busy checking out new condos. The townhouse we lived in would not work for me; it had many steps and the bedrooms were all upstairs or in the basement. He found a first-floor condo without any steps that had two rooms, two bathrooms, one study room, and a one-car garage. All the doors inside were wide enough for my wheelchairs. The only problem was a low step to enter the shower room. Swallowing his pride on behalf of his son, he reached out to one of the church deacons who was a professional contractor. He gladly came and fixed the problem.

After three months of rehab at Craig Hospital, I was finally home. Even though it was a new home, the presence and welcome of my parents and Jaelong, our dog who had been part of our family for the past seven years, was enough to call it home. It took some time to get used to the new environment. Unlike at Craig Hospital where everything was modified to meet the needs of people with spinal cord injuries, the condo was not built for people with disabilities. As my dog was sniffing around the new condo, I tried to get used to the new environment in my wheelchair. I made sure that I could enter and maneuver my chair in bedrooms, bathrooms, the kitchen, and garage, and checked to see if I could open the front door, bedroom and bathroom doors, and kitchen cabinets. It was perfect. My new journey as a quadriplegic started at that new condo.

Blood Clots

As I was slowly adapting to the new environment, I observed something different about my right thigh. It was bigger than the left thigh and swollen. My parents and I tried to remember any incident that might have hurt my right leg, but we sensed that something was wrong and called Craig Hospital. One of the nurses told me to go to the emergency room located in downtown Denver as soon as possible because she suspected it was a sign of a blood clot. I was eventually seen by an emergency doctor who saw my thigh and ordered an ultrasound. Blood clots had developed in that area, and after the doctor diagnosed deep vein thrombosis (DVT), he ordered an operation as soon as possible.

Soon thereafter, I was on a hospital bed for surgery looking at the ceiling. Unlike my previous surgery at St. Mary's Hospital, this time there were a few medical students in the operation room. Also unlike the last time, I was under a partial anesthesia and somewhat conscious of the conversation that the surgeon was having with her medical students. I heard the students laughing and the surgeon talking about my spinal cord injury. I felt a bowl movement on the operation table and was aware of the surgeon cleaning after me and of the students laughing about something. At the end of the surgery the surgeon placed a filter in my inferior vena cava (IVC) to help prevent another DVT by catching and stopping blood clots from moving into my heart or lungs.

The time at the hospital was not too bad. I was given Oxycontin for my pain, and it felt good. It was like I was swimming in the ocean or high on ecstasy. When its effect wore off the next day and pain came back, nurses gave me more of the magical experience. That might be why the time at the hospital had gone smoothly despite being confined to the hospital bed since I didn't have my electric wheelchair.

I wondered how much the medical bills would cost this time. I had been praying to God for healing and many of my needs during rehab at Craig Hospital. "Lord, how will I pay for the medical bills?" A social worker had taken my CICP card, but I did not think it covered the cost of a hospital stay. On the day of my discharge, the social worker came to the room and handed me the card along with medical bills and paperwork. As soon as I saw the bill, I was surprised and asked her, "So where is the rest of the bill?" I couldn't believe that was all. There had to be hidden fees or additional medical bills coming in the mail. But she assured me that while the total amount was $75,000, because of my CICP card, I received a significant discount. I owed the hospital only $100. This time Dad understood our conversation without any confusion and we both expressed our appreciation to her. We looked at each other and could not believe that CICP was that beneficial and helpful.

Later that day, a nurse and doctor came to my room to explain more about my situation and give me my discharge instructions. She explained again that the filter that had been inserted would prevent any remaining or new blood clots from traveling up to my lungs, heart, or brain. She told me I needed to take blood-thinning medication and see a doctor regularly to monitor the thickness of my blood. She also explained that a DVT was a common condition for people with a spinal cord injury. I remembered that the nurses at Craig Hospital had told me about this and had given me a shot in my belly every day. She confirmed that this would have been a blood thinner, but was surprised to learn that I had not been prescribed a blood thinner after I was discharged. She told me to talk to the doctor later and start taking the blood thinning medication.

I was confused by the fact that my primary doctor at Craig had forgotten to prescribe the blood-thinning medication. If I hadn't gotten to the hospital right away, I could have died from a heart attack or stroke. Everything worked out, but did God know that all these things would happen and use Lucy and Dad to get the card before I was discharged from Craig? Soon after, Dad came into the room and we wheeled out of the hospital. I was glad to have been treated there but I wondered whether it was the end of coming to the hospital for other issues related to my spinal cord injury.

Mounting Medical Bills

I was home again, finally. And bills did begin to arrive about a month later, but not from that hospital stay. Bills from a surgeon's office, internal medicine doctor, hospital respiratory department, ski patrol, ambulance, and radiology department from my accident finally arrived. I never knew that medical services were so expensive. At first there were only about five bills, but as weeks passed by, I began receiving dozens of bills demanding payments with warnings that unpaid bills would be transferred to collection agencies, which many were. In addition to the letters, there were at least one to three calls a day, and most were from the collection agencies.

One collection agent and I had a challenging conversation. He asked me why, if I had a phone and internet and ate three meals a day, couldn't I pay my bills? I explained that I had a disability and wanted to pay the bills, but I could not work, let alone move my body. It was too much to explain that I did not receive any financial aid and could not rely on my parents to help with the bills. But he accused me of lying about my condition and that angered and humiliated me. I did not appreciate his accusation that I was a liar and a fraud. But then again, what did I expect from a collection agent who was just doing his job? Did I expect sympathy from him? I thought for a moment and then laughed because deep down I realized that I actually did want him to understand my situation and expected sympathy from him, even though it was his job to collect the payment from his client.

The lovely calls and letters woke me up to face my reality. I knew I had to do something about them. People with a spinal cord injury, I was told, were able to receive different types of support from the government. When I was doing my rehab at Craig Hospital, Lucy tried to help me access those benefits, but I was not qualified to receive them because of my immigration status. I did not understand the qualifications and purposes of the government supports but I applied for Social Security Disability Insurance, Medicaid, Medicare, Vocational Rehabilitation, and the Food Stamp Program, despite having no clue about these programs.

"I am sorry. You are not qualified for this program. Please check other programs." This was the common response I received. I tried again and reached out to other organizations which were associated with helping people with disabilities. My applications were rejected; my pleas were declined; I was not qualified to receive their help according to their standards because I was not a legal permanent resident or American citizen. I could not blame them because those programs were established by the US government to support its permanent residents and citizens. The government was not a charity organization.

Yet every time my application was rejected, I could not help feeling that the rejection was personal. Whenever I met a social worker or government employee in person to explain my application and situation and to appeal the rejections, I found myself attempting to arouse sympathy from the interviewers who had no power to change the government policy. I was so desperate that I was willing to beg for financial funding. At first, I thought, "Hey, where is your freaking pride? Do you see yourself? You are pathetic. Even with your disability, you had your pride. Now, you are selling your pride for money." These thoughts only made me more miserable.

There I was, an Asian minority living in the US with a physical disability with no legal status to live in, work in, or receive any support from this country. I had a GED but no college degree. I had no source of income and no insurance compensation and I had a lot of debt. I had no job and no ability to work anytime soon. I had no special skill I could use to work while being in a wheelchair with paralysis. I had saved about $20,000 over the years, which I thought was a lot of money, but it evaporated by paying legal fees and medical expenses. I had no family member or friend or relative rich enough to take care of the hospital bills.

Who was I? I thought that I was just like the other patients at Craig. We had similar injuries but different living conditions and hardships. I thought that I was a Korean American just like my Korean American friends, but the US government did not think so. I guess I am just a Korean living in this country. I had already experienced bitterness and pain from the snowboarding accident. Now new negative thoughts came from being continuously rejected by many government programs and pursued by collection agencies. My mind, pride, dignity, identity, confidence, self-esteem, and life were broken like my body and were disabled. I would be categorized with the following "hashtags": disability, wheelchair, spinal cord injury, illegal immigrant, poverty, lower class, failure, lame, disability check, patient, debt, loser, dependence, cripple, victim, special need, handicap, limitations, unfortunate, and so forth. What a welcome to the real world!

Broken Family

In Korean culture, living with parents as a young adult until marriage was somewhat common, but American culture in the early 2000s considered the arrangement more shameful. Personally, I felt embarrassed that I had to move back to my parents' house, but there was no other option. I had to depend on them to survive.

Living with my parents again was not a glorious return as it would have been after graduating from college or after achieving something "great." It felt like a defeat from a war and the air in the house felt like a war zone. Mom often told Dad that if we hadn't come to the US, we would not have had all these troubles. She had told him many times over the years that they should go back to Korea. "Returning might have been hard, but anything would be better than this. At least our son wouldn't be in a wheelchair. This tragedy would not have happened." Dad usually just listened quietly. But there were other times when he got angry and shouted back at Mom and would walk outside. I usually listened to them without saying anything. I did not like hearing their arguments, but sometimes the quietness was even more daunting.

Mom was also upset with me. She wondered why I hadn't listened to her when she asked me to come back to Korea with her, to which I responded that I had been afraid of being bullied and ridiculed by classmates back in Korea if we had returned after only six months in America. Then she reminded me how tired Dad and she had been the night before my accident. She reminded me that she had begged me to sleep at home to give them some rest. I knew deep inside of me that if I had just stayed home that night, none of this would have happened.

People have spinal cord injuries for various reasons. Some people break their necks as a result of the mistakes of others or their own negligence. Others break their necks while serving their countries or from accidents. I broke my neck because I decided to enjoy my life and go snowboarding without thinking about the hardship it would cause my parents. I chose to leave the bar and drive to Aspen the night before the accident and to have fun with my friends. One way or the other, I made the choice and had to bear the responsibility whether I liked the outcome or not. The weight of the responsibility was heavy.

I was the offender who inflicted pain on the victim as well as the victim who had to suffer the pain inflicted by the offender. The offense was accidental and morally innocent. I did not mean to harm the victim. All I wanted to do was have fun with my friends. My parents were exhausted that night and ended up cooking for me without taking a break so that I could leave right away. My decision was selfish. But did I deserve such a punishment? I loved drinking and doing drugs, but I caused no harm to anybody except myself. The consequences of the offense were too cruel for the victim who would suffer the unbearable pain for the rest of his life. I was the offender and the victim. I had done this to myself and could not wrongly accuse anyone of the offense. A choice that seemed harmless brought harmful results to my family and me. Surely this is life.

Broken Church

Dad tried his best to serve the church. Before my accident, he led early morning services six days a week, plus the Wednesday service, Friday prayer meeting, and the Sunday worship service. On Saturdays he operated a Korean academy where he taught speaking and writing in Korean, Korean culture, and *Tae Kwon Do*. He picked up the students whose parents had to work on Saturdays and dropped them off afterward. He also ran an afterschool program on weekdays for middle school and high school students in the church. He picked them up after school, brought them to the church, helped them to do their homework, and dropped them off at home afterward because most of their parents worked and needed someone to take care of and supervise them. Dad was all-in with his ministries.

The first time I returned to the Sunday worship service after my discharge from Craig Hospital was to please Dad. I just wanted to stay home and did not want to meet anybody, but it was the least I could do for him. Many church members had visited me when I was at Craig, but I was somewhat anxious about seeing them again because I thought by then that I would be walking. When we arrived at church, Mom parked me in the large worship room and left me there to help Dad set up the lobby. While alone in the worship room, I contemplated what I would say to the church members I had known for at least four years.

But, something was different. It was fifteen minutes before the beginning of the worship service but nothing was set up, not even the chairs in the worship room. There weren't the usual sounds of greetings and conversation, no kids running around, and no people in the worship room except my parents and me. The worship service started without any church members present. I could not understand where the church members or deacons were. Two members showed up late and had a very short, awkward conversation with my parents afterward. For the next twelve months, the three of us were the only ones in the big worship room every Sunday. The emptiness in the room echoed the emptiness of our hearts and spirits. We later moved the service to a small fellowship room.

What I did not know was that about four months before my snowboarding accident, some issues arose at the church. A retired pastor who had been attending began meeting with church members behind Dad's back while he was busy taking care of me. They started their own church meetings and left Dad's church. While there had been issues that needed to be resolved between Dad and the retired pastor, since they were between them, he never expected their personal problems to lead to this type of breakup within the church. There was no judicial church process to resolve the issue, no attempt to pursue peace and unity in the church, and no sympathy and compassion for my parents who were fellow believers going through tremendous pain, frustration, and breakdown. Perhaps he had made some big mistakes and somehow made the congregation feel uncomfortable enough to leave the church.

After the members left the church, there was no reconciliation between Dad and the congregation. No former members visited us; no one was there to share my parents' burdens. There were no visitors either, which may have been just as well as there was no one who was able to greet them with an authentic smile. I thought that it was cruel for the congregation to leave their once-respected leader and pastor and fellow brother in Christ. Had they forgotten my parents' many sacrifices?

I did not hear anything from the church members who had met on a weekly basis for two to three years. Maybe they felt uncomfortable around me and thought my family was cursed by God or was receiving punishment from God for wicked, hidden sins and did not want to be associated with us. Whatever the reason, although I was not an ethical person in any position to judge them, I could not help judging and criticizing them. No, it was not about me getting support from them. Because I could not do anything for my parents, I hoped that someone else could offer them some kind of comfort or friendship and presence.

Did I expect too much from Christians? It seemed that even unbelievers who are not mandated to love others and be compassionate to those who go through hardships would not leave their leader, friend, or fellow human being in their most difficult circumstances. Even Mom's non-Christian customers offered their shoulders to cry on and their time to take care of her tailoring shop so that she could have few days off.

Thinking about the sorrow, anger, frustration, disappointment, and the feeling of betrayal that my parents could have felt at the moment broke my heart completely and caused me to be angry and hold a grudge against them. If church should never be this way, was it a church before? Was it disguised as a church under the banner of the cross, the melody of Christian music, and the preaching of the Word? No. Just because they were not there to support my parents doesn't mean that they were not believers or that it was not a church.

Many pastors who were affiliated with Dad's denomination, as well as the leadership of Trinity Baptist Church under which he was doing ministry, graciously provided us with prayers and financial support. But eventually the day came when Dad was no longer able to serve the church as the senior pastor. After doing his best to serve AKBC for a few years after my accident, he knew that it was a time to leave. This was the end of his role as the senior pastor of AKBC, but his passion and calling as a pastor remained deep in his heart and spirit.

Unwanted Responsibility

By this point, Mom was running a small tailoring shop, B. P. Tailor, in early 2004. She worked very hard and tried her best to serve her customers, most of whom loved her and the quality of her work. Even though Dad served as the senior pastor of AKBC, income from B. P. Tailor was the major source of my parents' income. With his unexpected retirement, there were no savings, we had no insurance, and no 401k. Without Medicaid it was too costly for us to hire a tech to help me. It is possible that we saved around $8,400 a month because Dad took on that role seven days a week and at least eight hours a day.

Although Mom wanted to be my caregiver at first, Dad decided to be my caregiver, believing that taking care of his son and doing anything he could to take care of his family was God's new mission for him. Making the transition from being a pastor to caregiver was somewhat challenging for him. Being born and raised in a traditional family background where a husband served as the main provider of his family, Dad felt badly that his wife had to bear the burden of earning for her family on her shoulders. However, my parents knew that this arrangement was the best way for our family to survive the harsh and challenging situation, and Dad was committed to putting aside traditional ideas and values to do whatever it took for the wellbeing of his family.

Dad helped me with everything, starting with helping me get ready in the morning to getting me ready for bed at night; both took about two hours. During the day he helped me take showers, use the toilet, changed urine bags and catheters, transferred me to the wheelchair in the morning and to bed at night, and gave me medications three times a day. In addition, he helped me with preparing lunch and often dinner for our family; filling my water bottle; turning on the computer in the morning; giving me rides; charging the battery for my wheelchair at night; and organizing my medications, supplies, books, bills, and desk. Right after the accident, when I had insufficient strength and needed twenty-four-hour care, he did even more for me. Taking care of me kept him very busy.

Getting used to this new arrangement in our relationship was not easy. Being taken care of by Dad and depending on him with more private activities was somewhat embarrassing and uncomfortable. I was certain that he felt uncomfortable too, but there was no time or room for such feelings. It was a matter of survival. No one else was there to help us. If Dad did not help me get out of bed, I would be stuck in bed all day. I had no options, and both of us knew it. I kept telling myself that I shouldn't feel embarrassed because Dad loved me very much. Instead, I should be grateful that I had a full-time caregiver, and that he was willing to help me with all my needs.

In addition to feeling uncomfortable about having Dad as my caregiver, we experienced physical difficulties that occurred due to his way of caregiving because he was not a professional caregiver. Although he tried his best to help me, I found myself unsatisfied with his best efforts and even complained, and my impatience got the best of me many times. Dad was very understanding and never responded with irritation or frustration. There were times when I asked him for too many things, and he was irritated by me many times, but yet he still got all of them for me. Over time we began to understand each other.

My Parents' Spiritual Crisis

From my observation over the years, my parents were devout Christians. Mom was the spiritual pillar or matriarch of my family. She became a believer in her middle school years and married Dad, who grew up in a

Buddhist and Confucianism background and only went to church a few times with his elementary school friends during holiday seasons to receive special gifts. Dad's mom found out about it and stopped him from going to church. Mom prayed for his conversion with tears every morning and night. He became a Christian when I was four years old. After a few years, my grandparents and great-grandmother became believers and everyone got rid of all household items related to other religions. After that they were all-in for Jesus. They participated in discipleship trainings and Bible studies and attended many Christian seminars and revival services.

Before moving to the US, Mom led small groups and discipleship programs. Dad volunteered as a youth group director and drove a bus on Sundays to help the elderly church members. He ran an afterschool program and had twenty teachers and two hundred students. God blessed my parents with faith, joy, gratitude, and wealth. They often told me that it was the best time of their lives. When they immigrated to America, they continued practicing their faith in God. It was in this context that they heard that their son may never walk again in his life.

I could not imagine what my parents were going through after their son became like a child, dependent upon them to be fed, cleaned up after, and helped with daily life. They felt helpless in their inability to help their son move again and bear the burden that he was bearing. Mom often lamented in her tears, "Son, I am sorry that I cannot help you and that I cannot suffer for you. I am so sorry for your suffering." She was sorry for my suffering, yet I was the one who had been so selfish as to leave home that night to have fun with my friends. I was the one who chose to move to Aspen despite their advice to stay in Denver, and who broke her heart numerous times by forsaking her love and taking for granted her wisdom and encouragement throughout my life. Dad did not say too much, but in his prayers, I heard his tears and felt his agony.

My parents devoted their lives to God and believed that God would remember their sacrifices and faith and deliver their son who had walked away from God. Having seen me living a worldly lifestyle and having their expectations shattered at a young age, they did not expect too much from God. It was not that they did not believe that God could bring good things through my life, they simply wanted me to be a faithful Christian without causing any more trouble or hurting myself. When they saw me getting promotions as a sushi chef, saving money, and calling them often, they saw these as signs that God was finally working in me and answering their prayers. However, what they heard from my doctor was far from good news and completely different from the message of their Lord and Savior who healed the lame and paralytic as recorded in the Bible. At the very least, the accident should not have happened and God should have prevented it. Their faith was in crisis.

Part 5

New Life with God

Nothing was changing. I put my hope in rehabilitation, stretches, acupuncture, and the latest developments in stem cell research, yet I still couldn't walk. It was keeping me from pursuing my dreams and goals. This was not what I wanted for my life. I wanted to care for my parents, not be cared for by them. We were learning to adapt to my limitations, but it was a daily struggle. There seemed to be only one thing left to do: give God a shot. What could it hurt?

Broken Hope to Walk Again

After the snowboarding accident, despite the fact that the doctor had said my chances of walking again were unlikely, I tried everything I could to move my body. First I tried rehabilitation. After being discharged from Craig Hospital, I tried to move my arms and legs and to stimulate the damaged nerves by continuously moving them just as the physical and occupational therapists had trained me. One of my friends' mother who was training to be a physical therapist helped me with stretching and physical therapy daily for some time. However, after a year or so, nothing changed in my body. I had no new movement.

Next I tried acupuncture. The logic behind trying acupuncture was to improve blood circulation and nerve regeneration. Dad took me to an acupuncture specialist every week; the treatment was helpful for blood circulation and muscle relaxation, but it didn't regenerate the severed nerves. A Korean pastor who was an acupuncture specialist also visited me occasionally. He told us that there was a special green needle made with a natural substance which dissolved when inserted into a human body. According to him, his research project with the natural needle was being researched at one of the universities in California. He often brought the needles and inserted them on my neck near the spinal cord injury area, explaining to me that the needles could help the broken nerves regenerate when they dissolved. It sounded somewhat reasonable at the time, so we had him come to my house and practice the green needle treatment. I had to do something—and doing something was better than nothing—but it didn't work and also made my neck very uncomfortable. I could not help feeling disappointed at its failure to help me.

Finally, I tried a roasted grain diet program that was very popular in South Korea for people with diabetes, heart disease, and so forth in 2005 and 2006. Roasted grains contain B vitamins, which are known for having the potential to regenerate nerves—although not specifically for spinal cord nerves. A friend living in Korea sent us many boxes of roasted grain. The company that promoted this diet also provided special instructions for following it, which I followed religiously. However, it restricted its participants from eating any type of meat and processed food, even chicken and fish. I was a meat lover, so the program was torture for seven months, but it was worth pursuing if I wanted to walk again. I watched as my family ate dinner without me. It was hard but also satisfying to see them eat what I could not.

During those seven months I lost about thirty pounds and looked pale and unhealthy. I had no energy or strength. I often fainted during showers due to low blood pressure. When I talked for more than three minutes, I felt fatigued and often fainted. As I was not getting any new movement, I stopped the roasted grain diet before it further damaged my life, but not before my hope was damaged again. My disappointment over my lack of improvement was deeper and much more painful than anything I had experienced before.

Sometime in 2005, I heard promising news concerning stem cell research. A South Korean researcher named Hwang Woo-Suk published research articles and reported that he had succeeded in creating human embryonic stem cells in his research trials. Ever since my snowboarding accident, I had been interested in stem cell research because only stem cells could help regenerate my severed spinal cord nerves. My family and I were exuberant. The researcher was praised among South Koreans as the "pride of Korea." I also thought that he was appointed by God to heal me. As I prayed to God for healing, I also prayed for and put a lot of hope in this stem cell research.

But after a few months of waiting, instead of the good news that we had been expecting, it was reported that the researcher had used human embryonic stem cells for research projects which was a violation of ethics. Soon after, an investigation found that his research project was completely fraudulent. Many people who had put their hope in his research felt the world crashing down on them. Stem cell research had given them new meaning and a purpose to live, courage to hope and dream again, and served as light in their darkness and valleys of shadow of death.

When my primary doctor told me that I may not walk for the rest of my life, I understood the severity of the spinal cord injury. Still, I had hope in science and medicine. We have advanced science and technology to travel to the moon and develop iPhones and Galaxy phones. What about medicine? We have incredible doctors and medical science to treat many diseases that were once incurable. We now have cars that operate without using any oil and sufficient technology to develop fancy wheelchairs which have options of tilting, reclining, and even standing. What isn't possible in the name of science? However, I understood that science was not able to solve my problem at that moment. Perhaps it could in the future, but at least in 2006, I knew it wasn't the solution. But I was disappointed because I had thought God would use science to heal my spinal cord injury and that it would lead to me being able to walk again.

All of my efforts failed. Each time I hoped for something, I was disappointed. When failure continued and the mileage of disappointment reached this point, my hope was shattered. I wanted to put the broken pieces together to hope again but was afraid of cutting myself on the sharp edges. To hope became fear. Stem cell research used to be the hope that moved my paralyzed spirit and filled the loss of my joy and happiness. So much emptiness overwhelmed me. I tried to stay positive as if nothing happened, but it was not a good feeling or experience. I consoled myself that at least I had tried my best. There was nothing else I could do to change my condition.

I told myself to cheer up because I still had God, so that there was no reason for me to be disappointed. As I was wishing that such a thought and attitude would encourage me, it lingered in my thoughts for some time and helped me to see the positive side of hope again and to hope in my best option. The power of hope gradually calmed the storm in me, the hope that

God is alive and is able to heal me without using any means, just like the way he restored the sight of people with blindness as recorded in the Bible

Assignment One: Reading the Bible

While my parents' relationship with God was in jeopardy, my journey with God was just beginning, although it was uncertain at that time. As the saying goes, desperate people do desperate things; whatever my belief was at the moment of my decision to call out to God and try religion as a means to receive my healing, I made a desperate choice. I felt as if I was drowning. I made a dangerous decision; it was all or nothing. I decided to go all-in for Jesus and to give everything I had.

I had to think about what it meant to go all-in and do "Christian" things. Many ideas were flowing in my mind, and four of them became very clear and appealing to me, as if God was giving me assignments that demanded personal commitment. First I began reading the Bible. I had never been a fan of reading anything aside from comic books, let alone the Bible. I knew that reading the Bible was a very important part of living a Christian life and a command decreed by God; I knew many Bible stories, but I also knew that the Bible was thick and boring. However, my parents enjoyed it and tried to read through the entire Bible every year. I thought I would give it a try because reading the Bible was a Christian thing to do and I thought God would give me credit for my effort. That was the attitude that I had before reading the Bible and it also shows how much I wanted to walk again. Maybe God was moving my heart to spend time with him.

But I ran into an immediate problem: I had no desk at which to read the Bible. I needed a special desk or table for my wheelchair, but the table we had was too short and narrow for my wheelchair. I had not thought to ask my occupational therapist where to purchase an adjustable desk for reading books and using a computer. We had to get creative until we could find a special desk. Dad put a wooden sliding board on top of both sides of the armrests of my wheelchair, then affixed a sticky pad on the board, and finally put the Bible on the pad. It worked, but I had to lower my head so much that my neck was very painful. Dad then put two phone books (Yellow Pages) on the board, replaced the sticky pad and the Bible, and there was my first desk. It looked (and was) very unstable. If I bumped it, the Bible would fall on the floor. And when I had to tilt my wheelchair, I had to hold both phone books and the Bible to prevent them from falling on the floor. My body was uncomfortable, but despite my limited movement using typing sticks, I slowly turned the pages of the Bible.

At first, after thirty minutes of reading, I had to take a break. But when I gained more strength, I could read for an hour and more. However, this led to more body and neck pain because of my awkward reading posture. So Dad brought home a long white rectangular plastic table that he used for church fellowship and put two bricks under the four corners of the table to adjust the height of the table. In that way, I was able to park my wheelchair under the table and put books on the table; however, I still needed a book stand to read a book without having more neck pain. Despite not being gifted at carpentry and making things with his hands, Dad made a book stand using a thick paper box. It was perfect, and we said goodbye to the phone books. I was finally able to read the Bible without discomfort.

I decided to spend at least two hours reading the Bible every day. Unlike students or other people who had a part-time or full-time job, I had plenty of time to kill. My parents recommended reading the whole Bible from the beginning to the end, Genesis to Revelation. Thus, my first goal was set, and I was driven to do this thinking that a special experience would occur when I finished reading the whole Bible.

Reading Genesis and its many stories was somewhat exciting and enjoyable, but after I finished the first half of Exodus, I felt drowsy. I kept on, and after enduring Exodus with all my heart, strength, and spirit, I faced an even higher mountain: Leviticus and Numbers. My mind was soon filled with questions. For example, what was the significance of the measurements of the inside of the temple, the colors of the clothes of the priests and the high priest, the numbers of the descendants of the twelve tribes of the Israelites, and the various types of sacrifices, feasts, and laws? Were they some sort of secret code that I needed to solve for their true meaning? Should I just skip these books and move on to the next one? I did not understand why they were included in the Holy Scriptures but I kept reading the Bible to complete my first mission.

About two months passed by and I reached the last page of Revelation. I was so excited to finish reading the whole Bible, expecting that God would send his angels to congratulate me or show me some sort of vision or glory for my faithfulness. When I read the last sentence, closed my eyes, and said "Amen," nothing happened. I opened my eyes to see whether there was anything different about my body or my surroundings, but they were the same. I laughed. What did I think would happen? If everyone received healing and experienced supernatural power after reading the Bible, who would not be a believer? The whole world would already be Christianized. Still, I felt satisfaction over completing my mission, and that satisfaction led me to spend two to three hours a day reading the whole Bible three to four times a year for the next few years. Although I still could not walk again, the satisfaction led me to love reading God's words.

True Repentance

Prior to reading the Bible, I wondered if doing certain things that did not harm anybody were really sins. Smoking cigarettes or going to parties did not hurt anybody. What was so bad about doing activities that made me happy? I make the choices that I wanted for my body, life, and future. Besides, I reasoned, there are too many laws in the Bible. Who could really live like that? Even if one could, I did not want to live a boring life. I would enjoy my life for a while, then maybe later when I was older I would go back to church and settle down.

With this type of attitude and perspective on sin, when I read the stories of the people who sinned against God and broke his covenant, at first I did not connect their stories to myself directly or personally. But as I read the Bible, feelings of heavy burden and guilt filled my heart. Over time I began remembering all the sins that I committed in the past. An amazing and scary part was that my sins were passing in the forms of images in my head. It was uncomfortable and even frightening to see the images of my sins against God and others. All of a sudden, without feeling sentimental or intending to cry, I became tearful. Discomfort gradually became pain, which intensified as I kept seeing myself doing wrong things. Was the pain that I experienced the pain that others felt when I wronged them? Could it be pain that God experienced with them or that he felt when I sinned against them or that God was inflicting on me as the consequence of my wrong deeds?

I didn't know, but one thing was clear: I realized that I was a sinner who had sinned against God and people. I could not grasp the degree of my sins. But on that special day, God did something in my heart, and I realized that I had messed up. I lived a wrong lifestyle. The Bible revealed my sinful nature that I intentionally and unintentionally had tried to hide from others, and even from myself. I did it so well that my friends, family, and co-workers were manipulated by my devious efforts and I, too, was so oblivious of my true nature that I often felt that I was too innocent and worthy to go through any hardships. A few of the sins of my worldly lifestyle included being prideful, selfish, sexually immoral, and abusive toward my body. I was jealous and envious of those who were successful. I disobeyed the commands and advice of my parents and did not appreciate their love and compassion. I took advantage of their love and neglected my relationship with them. I lied to and manipulated my friends and co-workers and others to get what I needed and wanted. I harmed people physically, verbally, and emotionally, and caused them so much pain. I also struggled with greed, gluttony, deception, selfish ambition, anger, and stubbornness.

That was who I had been all my life. I could not deny that any more than I could deny being in a wheelchair and my disability. I felt as if I were naked and in need of covering. Was I trying to magnify my sins? Did I want to show God that I, a horrific sinner, finally understood the depth of my sins and was finally kneeling under his throne to repent and to ask forgiveness? Did I want to persuade God that I learned my lesson and was ready to live a new life and to receive healing, as if God were somehow testing and training me for a moment? Yes, yes, and yes. However, I engaged in repentance authentically and sincerely in order to receive forgiveness from God. Furthermore, repentance happened supernaturally and miraculously, without hard work or resistance. That was the only explanation considering my stubbornness and arrogance. I became an avid and earnest repentant who was in desperate need of God's forgiveness. God did not regenerate my body, but he regenerated my broken mind.

Restored Family

When I was listening to a sermon concerning sin, the pastor preached that people need to ask the people they sinned against for their forgiveness. The message was somewhat of a shock to me because I had been so concerned with begging God's forgiveness that I had never thought of asking people to forgive my wrongdoings. As I thought about the people I had wronged, I thought especially of my parents who had been suffering because of my selfish decisions and irresponsible actions which had caused so much pain for them, from our move to this country to the time of my snowboarding accident on December 13, 2004. At that moment, I realized that I had never had a serious conversation with them about the accident or the ways that it had caused so much trouble and so many challenges for them. I always felt a lot of pain and sorrow for them and was sincere in my gratitude for their love and sacrifice. Deep inside of me, I felt the tension of needing to share my heart but also my resistance to doing so. I thought that they surely understood how I felt about the situation without having to tell them in person. Perhaps I felt somewhat embarrassed to apologize and admit my mistakes and wanted to cover up my faults.

During that moment of hesitation the Holy Spirit worked within me. He softened my hardened heart and turned it toward them so that I could ask them for a family meeting. That evening, as I was about to begin my confession of apology, I was so overwhelmed with pain and guilt that I could barely speak a word. Eventually I was able to tell them how sorry I was for disobeying them during my middle school and high school years in particular and for crushing their hearts, hopes, and love. I was sorry for all the trouble I'd caused over the years, and for not appreciating and understanding their love for me. I also shared how sorry I was to have caused all of the burdens that they were bearing for me physically, spiritually, and financially after the snowboarding accident, of taking responsibility as parents, and for loving their son in action and truth. I may never understand my parents' pain in seeing me go through various hardships. I thanked them with all my heart and with words that were insufficient to describe their love and sacrifice, and humbly asked for their forgiveness. I felt no shame, humiliation, or frustration. Actually, the more I said these words through tears and snot, the more warmth and freedom I felt within me.

After my confession, all of a sudden, Dad broke down and began sharing his side of the story. It was surprising to hear this conservative and stubborn Korean man sharing his regrets and mistakes with us. What shocked me was his confession: "I am sorry that I cannot provide more for you." As Dad was my full-time caregiver, I could not ask for more than what he was already doing; as father and husband, he was already doing his best for us, but yet he felt sorry for not being able to do more. At the same time, he said that he was sorry that he hadn't been more understanding when I was lost during my adolescent years. Dad and I had been like enemies; at least that was how I had thought of him because he considered everything that I wanted to do worldly and sinful. At that moment, there was a spirit-filled reconciliation between us.

Mom had begun crying as she heard my repentance and confession and her husband's heart and tears. Through tears, she told me that she was sorry for my hardships and that she could not suffer my pain for me. She wished she could do more and had more to support me with. Though she was already sacrificing so much to help me, like Dad, she felt that what she was sacrificing was not enough.

The Holy Spirit bound us in God's love and in our love for each other, and my family has never been the same. From that moment on, our appreciation, gratitude, respect, joy, and love has grown daily in the Lord, and we started expressing those sentiments more frequently, although it was not easy at first. We also began focusing on the present and our future without looking back on memories of the past and complaining about our hardship. Instead, we acknowledged, accepted, and assessed our challenges together; we talked about them to figure out appropriate strategies and solutions; we laid them before God and prayed both individually and communally.

We started having a weekly family prayer night. We sang two songs, Mom prayed, Dad shared a short message and presented specific issues and prayer requests, we prayed together out loud, and then we ended our meeting with the Lord's Prayer. My parents and I, as brothers and sisters in Christ, have come to have a wonderful relationship. We care for, pray for, and love each other. We are able to talk to each other about any issue and agree and disagree with each other in unity and love. My parents became my best friends, even though the concept of friendship with parents is still being developed in Korean culture. I often wondered if I could be like Dad if I had a selfish and arrogant son who had a disability? Could I give up my passions and sacrifice my time, strength, and life?

We did not have much financially. Mom's business was somewhat slow; there was no retirement plan for Dad; I had no income, savings, insurance compensation, government support, or job. We had to trust in God and each other. After paying the mortgage and living expenses, medical bills and supplies, and paying back money that we had borrowed, not much was left. We tried to save as much as possible and yet we were satisfied with what God had given us and were content in him.

Mom occasionally had her own health issues, and the only way to be appropriately examined by medical doctors was to go to the emergency room operated by University of Colorado Hospital. My family was enrolled in CICP because the health insurance was too expensive for us to afford. The problem with having to go to the ER for treatment was that since the hospital served people with low income just like my family, the wait time was very long. After packing books, a few water bottles, and bags of chips, we usually went to the ER on Saturday around 2:00 p.m. and came home around 12:00 a.m. or later, depending on the number of the patients. Though we waited many hours, we passed the time praying for each other and were grateful that we could still receive medical services. We were united in one God as one happy family. That was all that mattered, and we considered the time in the ER like a family picnic.

Assignment Two: Memorizing Verses

After reading the Bible, the second assignment God gave me was memorizing Bible verses. It seemed random because such a desire could only have been inspired by my desperation to walk again, by God's work within my heart, or by having seen my parents memorize and recite Bible verses aloud. My parents followed a Christian program called the Navigators which emphasized memorizing Bible verses. It started with memorizing sixty topical Bible verses and offered sixty small Bible memorization cards. On each card was written a topical Scripture in Korean and English and one card a week was to be memorized for the next sixty days or so.

I followed the same memorization program, but memorizing even one verse on a weekly basis was difficult. The challenge was retaining the verses that I thought I had memorized. Memorization meant more than just memorizing verses and moving to the next. It was a repeated process of memorizing and reciting them over and over or else I would forget them with lightning speed. I wondered if this was the effect of alcohol and drugs on my brain over the years. Having difficulty with organizing the small cards, I asked Dad to tape them all on the wall near my table so that I could see and recite them as often possible.

After two to three months passed by, I had memorized the sixty verses in Korean. I also felt the desire to memorize them in English, and within three months, I completed that task. I felt such a great sense of achievement and satisfaction and again expected God's rewards because it is written in the Bible that those who delight in and meditate on God's words will be blessed like "a tree planted by streams of water, which yields its fruit in season and whose leaf does not wither—whatever they do prospers" (Ps 1:3). I also learned that the word "meditate" in Hebrew means to recite and to read. I thought I was obeying God's words and that the day of being planted by the streams of water and yielding fruits in my seasons would come.

Interestingly, I did not want to stop memorizing Bible verses because I experienced peace and comfort in reciting them. I do not know if it was simply a feeling of satisfaction in completing the plan; I could not tell where the peace and comfort came from, but I found myself searching for more Bible verses that I liked and added them to my list. The number of verses gradually increased. One day, Mom told me how she was blessed by memorizing Romans 8, so I added those chapters to my list, which had grown to about three hundred verses.

I learned that the best way to memorize the verses was through repetition until the content was transferred from my short-term memory to my long-term memory. That meant that I had to consistently recite them. I also needed a memorization plan. I organized the Bible verses into three categories. In the first category was verses that I had already memorized. Verses that needed more repetition were in the second category. And new verses were in the third category. I recited the new verses daily whenever possible, whether I was in the car or outside, and when I reclined my wheelchair. I recited the verses in the second category twice a week, and the verses in the first category once every two weeks.

I remembered how my parents and their small Bible study group members used to gather and recite Bible verses together. They would share their burdens and the difficulty of memorizing Bible verses with each other, pray together, and share testimonies of experiencing God's blessing and of the joy of meditating on Scripture. I wished I had such a community and support from other believers and friends. Since I didn't have a group like that to share with, I thought perhaps I had done enough. But as this thought depressed me further, I challenged and pushed myself to keep at it. Over a few years of repetition, I was able to memorize about three hundred verses.

Winning Battles

My mind was a battleground. I was constantly battling with and defending my faith from my own negative thoughts. I wondered what the point was of reading about the Old Testament lifestyles, temple structure, and different methods of sacrificing. I was tempted to skip those parts. I knew that Mark, Matthew, and Luke had similar content, so what was the point of reading the repetitive parts? I'd already read the whole Bible few times and thought maybe I could stop reading it. I questioned whether I believed everything in the Bible. As a rational person, could I really believe that God split the Red Sea and that Jesus fed thousands with only five loaves of bread and two fish? Did I believe things that couldn't be explained scientifically?

Could I believe the things that I didn't understand? Faith, reason, experience, doubt, confusion, anxiety, misunderstanding, and frustration often screamed like a boiling tea kettle.

Again, I tried to think positively. I told myself that these were attacks from my sinful nature and the devil and not to be fooled. But these thoughts constantly filled my head. I tried reciting Bible verses to refute them. It did not work at first, but as I continued reciting them and praying to God, the loud voices and thoughts gradually softened and faded away, as if they never happened, although they came back in different forms and tricks. Surely the words of God were my sword against my enemies.

In this journey of wrestling with memorizing Bible verses, I was living with the words of God. When dwelling on a depressing thought, the words of hope filled my heart and cast away darkness. The promises made me confident that I was praying to the living God of Scripture. When battling temptation, the powerful words fought the battles for me. I could not deny that the words were my joy and peace which came from God, just like King David who wrote that meditating on the words of God is sweeter than honeycomb. At the same time, I sensed not only my faith maturing, but also my pride. I considered myself a faithful and sincere Christian.

Assignment Three: Reflection

The third assignment God gave me was to write a reflection after reading the Bible. When I started reading it, I wanted to underline verses that seemed meaningful, incomprehensible, encouraging, and questionable. I put a pen on my universal cuff and used it to underline verses in the Bible and to write short comments. But there wasn't enough room in the margins, so I began taking notes in a notebook. Writing short comments was tiring for my arms, but slowly they strengthened as if I was doing occupational therapy. For the first time in my life, I actually used a whole notebook! When I was a high school student, I had only ever used the first few pages of a new notebook. As short comments became longer, it took more time and energy to write with my limited arm strength. And my handwriting was so bad that there were times I could not read it. It was finally time to take another step, which was to use a laptop. I put two typing sticks on my hands and slowly began using the laptop with a touch pad. Typing was much faster and more effective than writing by hand and it also served as exercise when I had to type for a long time.

I often had depressing thoughts and did not feel much gratitude or joy in my life. I frequently wondered if I could be happy again unless I could move again. But one day I felt the desire to write a daily reflection based on my daily reading and interpretation of the Bible, but was hesitant to do it. I wondered if it was arrogant of me to write my own reflection since I thought that was a job for pastors. But since I wasn't planning to be a pastor or share my writing with others, I figured I had nothing to lose. Reading the Bible by itself was already a huge step for me, so writing a reflection seemed unthinkable. But without having to worry about the quality of my reflection or the pressure of receiving criticism or a grade, I could freely interact with my reason, imagination, experience, and faith. I spent more time reading, reflecting, and researching the Scriptures.

I was surprised to discover that I actually had many thoughts and questions and that I was actually interacting with and having a conversation with God. He would speak to me through his Word, and I responded in obedience. This time of reflection and writing became my favorite part of each day. His words were so calm, encouraging, and exciting that I could not get enough. Laying down my worry, fear, stress, and problems, I focused on God; I sought him and was found by him.

I also began to experience joy in reading and reflecting on his words and spending time with him. It was a joy that I had never experienced before. It was different from the pleasures of the world, going to parties and on vacations, playing golf, or hanging out with friends. It was calm and warm, as if I were laying on a white beach under a blue sky. Sometimes the joy felt like fireworks of dopamine filling every part of my body, soul, and spirit in perfect balance. It was clear, not confusing or lethargic. It was gentle and natural, not forceful. No worry, fear, or depression could penetrate the fortress of peace and joy; no lie or deception could twist the truths of the Word. I was often so fully immersed in the presence of God that I wanted to dwell in that moment for the rest of my life and wanted time and the world to stop.

After spending an hour or more in reading the Bible, I started reflecting on his words for hours and thought that I could do this all day long. I had never understood the Psalmist when he said that the word of God was sweeter than honeycomb. I thought he was exaggerating; I was wrong. The Psalmist did not go far enough in describing the joy of reflection on God's words. It was truly a miracle. I used to think that the Christian life without any drugs or alcohol was boring and I could not understand the smiles and happy faces of my parents and church members. Yet I became another fool in Christ.

I also started writing a personal journal. I wrote whatever crossed my mind and whatever I felt, thought, and experienced each day. As I put my worries, fears, disappointments, frustration, and anger in writing, I felt a release that was somewhat therapeutic and helpful. I could not afford to receive counseling and frankly did not think I needed it. However, this experience helped me to understand that releasing and expressing myself were positive and healthy practices and that counseling would not be too bad if it were not expensive.

Living in the Dead Dream

After about three months passed since I started journaling, I went to the first page of my journal to read what I had written. I was embarrassed by my own reflections. From the first day of journaling, there was a consistent theme that ran throughout the journal: "If I hadn't gone snowboarding that day I would be doing x, y, and z." I fed myself with regrets and unfulfilled dreams, particularly the "what ifs" of how my life would be different if the accident had not happened. This led to variations on the theme of how that day could have gone differently and even how past choices had led me to that point. Simultaneously, I daydreamed about the things that I wanted to accomplish if I didn't have a disability, such as continuing my pursuit of becoming a sushi chef at a renowned Japanese restaurant, going to parties and bars, finding an investor to start my own restaurant, and becoming rich and famous.

I magnified my past as if all the things that I had fantasized about might actually have happened. Could I really have become a head chef at Matsuhisa? Could I even have continued working as a sushi chef while drinking and doing drugs every day? Could I have saved more while spending more on my expensive habits? Could I have controlled myself to drive without the influence of alcohol or drugs and avoided hurting anybody? Could I have avoided getting into fights and trouble? Could I have continued working illegally using my friends' information without getting caught? I was playing the victim and justifying my daydreaming as if I had the right to do it all day.

My early dreams were behind me like a shadow. No matter how much I tried, I could not realize them. I had difficulty looking because I wondered how new dreams could compare to the dreams I had before. Then again, what if my new dreams were too high and noble for my reach? What if disability, a wheelchair, and paralysis were all part of the new dream? That would be a nightmare. I did not want to dream about living in a wheelchair, asking for the help of caregivers, and going through financial, medical, and physical hardships. Was I too scared to hope for a new dream?

There were actually many people with spinal cord injuries who seemed to move on with their lives rather quickly. I met David, who had a snowboarding accident in 2002 when he was a college student. He had a similar injury level and was paralyzed from his shoulders down. Six months after the accident and rehab at Craig Hospital, he decided to go back to his school and live in the dorm with his former roommates, who encouraged him to live with them and offered their help to him as caregivers. He later graduated and pursued his dream.

But I was still living in the past, repeatedly trying to resuscitate my dead dream. Deep inside of me, intellectually, I knew that I had to let go and get myself out of the past in order to take the next step forward. However, I was too eager to serve my needs and wants. My heart was not moving and was not persuaded that my old dreams were dead weight drowning my spirit. Daydreaming seemed to be a lifeboat, not dead weight. My dreams were like my baby which I nurtured, fed, sacrificed for, and spent many hours pursuing. It gave me joy, moved me every day, was part of my life, and defined my identity. Jettisoning it would be like abandoning my very self. There was nothing to replace it with. But I wondered what God thought about my daydreaming. Would he be pleased that I was chasing after a dead dream? Could I confidently share this with my loved ones? The answers were simple, but it was not easy to let my dreams go.

Daydreaming continued even while I was spending time with God in reading and reflecting on the Bible. It somehow relieved me of the pain of my broken body, life, and hope. In that world I was confident, alive, and happy; things I was not in the real world. It shifted my focus from the present problems to the dreams that I had wanted to accomplish. It was actually fun to dwell on the past and the chains of "what ifs." Did I not see that the things I was daydreaming about were merely the broken pieces of my dreams that I was trying to reassemble? Perhaps I was not ready to accept the truth. Perhaps I wanted my old dreams so much that even holding onto a few shards of the broken dreams gave me comfort. Maybe it was less painful than facing the reality and dark future that I knew was ahead, not realizing that my hands were bleeding and that I needed to let go of the broken pieces.

The Final Assignment: Prayer

The last assignment was to pray to God, and as I simply wanted to walk again, I prayed to God for healing. I had prayed to God in the past, but if he had answered my prayers directly, I don't recall it. Having grown up as a PK, I had to participate in church retreats and special worship services such as revival nights. Dad often prayed in a language that I could not understand. Christian communities called it speaking or praying in tongues. I had heard such prayers spoken by my parents and their church friends and thought that they were mystical and fascinating. I thought that if I received the gift of speaking in tongues I would actually believe in the existence of God. When Dad led revival nights, I often asked God for this gift. Despite my lack of complete trust in him, I believed that God would hear my supplications and those of my faithful parents and pastors and heal me. My desire and desperation to walk again drove me to kneel in his presence and start my prayer life.

Dad stayed home in the mornings to take care of me for several months because I had insufficient strength to control my limited body movement. After I had gained enough strength to manage my body movements, he and I agreed that I would be safe at home without him watching over me for a few hours in the morning. After setting up my big phone that has large buttons, my Bible, and a water bottle, he turned on Christian music and went to Mom's business. When he was home, I prayed silently so that he would not hear my words. However, when I was home alone, I could freely express myself and my anger, frustration, sorrow, desperation, and remorse. I was finally able to be honest and express myself freely and safely without faking my smiles and diminishing my suffering for the sake of my beloved parents.

On the first day of being alone at home after the accident, Mom and Dad cheered for me as they walked out the front door and urged me to call Dad if anything happened, as though I were a child being left at home for the first time. I stationed my chair under the table and got myself ready for prayer. I slowly opened my mouth and said aloud, "Father God . . . please have mercy on me." These seven words were strong enough to open the floodgate of my heart and spirit. Tears flooded from my eyes and snot dripped down my nose; my words became cries. I no longer understood my words or tears. I was out of control, crying my heart out, as if my inner person took control of me. It was the cry of my heart that I had withheld for a long time. For a few days, the cry of my heart was my prayer to God. Finally, when I was able to pray to God using actual words, they were simple: "Lord have mercy on me! Heal me!" I cried out to God and screamed my lungs out. Pounding my chest, crying, and asking God for healing and provisions, I spent at least an hour in prayer daily until I was exhausted and my throat was too sore for further prayers.

While reading the Book of Daniel, I noticed that Daniel prayed to God three times a day. I decided to follow his example. Morning prayer was devoted to receiving God's healing, late afternoon prayer was dedicated to intercessory prayer for my loved ones and people around the world, and night prayer was for God's provision. But I felt that Daniel's prayer was not desperate enough, so I started my day with prayer and listening to sermons and Christian music and ended my day with prayer. Slowly, prayer became a regular part of my life. During times of prayer, my mind was often distracted by various thoughts. After five minutes of prayer, I found myself thinking about weird things out of nowhere. I tried harder to concentrate on prayer, but I found myself at the same place. So I started praying out loud, and this helped me concentrate on praying.

At night, the same thing happened. But this time I found myself thinking about doing worldly activities that I loved and would stay up all night; once the train of dreaming began, there was no end to my brain activity. Even when I wanted to stop, I could not fall asleep after thinking about it for hours. About two months later, I realized that I was sinning against God, just as Jesus taught that thinking about adulterous thoughts was equivalent to committing actual adultery (Matt 5:28). Even when I tried to stop, worldly thoughts simply invaded my mind and I was powerless to defend myself. "God help me to overcome these thoughts! Please fight the battle for me. I am too weak so I hide in your fortress." This became my prayer at night for days and weeks, and the thoughts no longer controlled me. After experiencing the power of prayer I dedicated more time and effort to it by making a daily schedule to maintain the pattern of prayer so that I would not simply quit after doing them for few days or weeks. I was committed to praying without giving up until the day I received healing from God. I was confident that it was the perfect recipe for healing.

No More Blame!

As I repeatedly thought about "what if" questions, I noticed that I held Sean somewhat responsible for my snowboarding accident. If only he had listened to me that night and we'd stayed at my house. Or if we had gone to more bars with our friends and gotten drunk instead of driving back to Aspen that night, that day would not have become the cursed day of mourning. I blamed him for my paralysis. Deep inside of me I needed a scapegoat—someone to blame for my ruined life. At the same time, I knew that I had made the decision to go snowboarding that day and had no right to accuse him of what happened. I struggled really hard to stop myself from blaming him and prayed to God for his help. Having lost a part of myself already, I resisted losing another important part of my life. I couldn't afford to lose my friend.

Thankfully, God answered my prayer by gradually transforming my negative attitude into gratitude for having a wonderful friend. About six months after my accident, although he had often told me that he was sorry about the accident, Sean cautiously mentioned that he had been dealing with guilt and sorrow over causing the accident, as if it was his fault. I told him that I did not blame him anymore and that what occurred on that day was an accident that nobody expected or wanted, and that he was not responsible for the challenges that I was experiencing. Thankfully, we were back on track.

This Is Your Day!

Later in 2005 I met one of Dad's pastor friends, Pastor Lee. He was a faithful servant of God, respected not only by his church's congregation but also by many Korean pastors in the Denver community. Although I was not a member of his church, he visited me weekly and prayed for my healing, which I respected. One day he recommended that I watch Christian television programs, including one called "This Is Your Day" led by Pastor Benny Hinn. Pastor Hinn traveled around the world and led big worship services which were called miracle crusades because miracles of healing happened during the services. He often taught on the Christian life, particularly about faith, healing, and miracles.

During the miracle crusades, Pastor Hinn preached the message of the gospel and prayed for the attendees. He often prayed for healing and shouted to them, "Be healed and receive the Holy Spirit!" After his prayer, many people would come up to the platform to share their testimonies of healing and miracles. When the pastor put his hand on individuals on the platform, they fell on the ground, as if God touched them. There were times when Pastor Hinn swung his hand towards the congregation, and dozens of people fell back on the ground without being touched. Later I learned that such a performance was called a spiritual swing or swing in the spirit.

What was my response to the television program and miracle crusades? *Eureka!* I had found the answer to my healing and prayer and fully believed that Pastor Hinn's miracle crusade was the ministry and work of the Holy Spirit. Pastor Lee had recommended the program and ministry, so I did not doubt the miraculous healing and work of the Holy Spirit. Pastor Hinn's sermons on God's power, healing, and our faith seemed biblical and convincing, and I interpreted them as God's personal and customized messages for me. He was scheduled to be in Denver to lead a miracle crusade on September 23, 2005. He was a busy man, traveling around the world, so such an event in Denver was a rare and once-in-a-lifetime experience. Therefore I believed it had to be some sort of divine appointment for my healing. It was my destiny to walk again. September 23, 2005 was my day.

As Pastor Hinn preached on the significance of having a strong faith in God and stressed that our faith could be strengthened through obedience, repentance, and sowing seeds of faith and finance, I intensified the level of my spiritual disciplines. I spent more time in prayer, reading the Bible, memorizing Bible verses, and reflecting on them. As he taught that our sins were the cause of our sickness and misfortunes, I repented of my sins, asked for forgiveness repeatedly, and examined carefully whether I had any unrepented or hidden sins in my heart. I stopped watching all television programs except Christian programs. When any doubt, fear, or worry visited my mind, I avoided thinking about it lest it, according to his teaching, weaken my faith. I needed a stronger faith. When I reclined my wheelchair and lay in bed, I imagined how I would respond to healing that day and what I would say to the pastor and cameras broadcasting to thousands of the viewers. I was getting ready for healing.

Finally, the weekend came for the miracle crusade. I was hoping to be healed on the first night, Friday night, but I didn't mind receiving healing on Saturday either. When I arrived hours early with Dad and Sean to get front-row seats, there were already dozens of people waiting outside.

Everyone was infused with hope, faith, and positive energy, and smiled at one another saying, "This is your day! This is your day for healing!"

At last the service began. There was worship, a sermon, and an offering taken, but I was just waiting for the last part of the event. Finally the pastor began praying for people with different types of illnesses and conditions. His prayer intensified as he yelled "be healed, be healed, be healed in the name of Jesus Christ!" All of a sudden Sean, who had elbow and hip injuries, began crying and stepping backwards. The pastor continued praying and Sean once again stepped backwards and almost fell behind. I wanted to experience the spiritual swing. As I saw him nearly fall back, I shifted my attention to prayer and cried out, "Lord, I am ready for the swing. I am ready for your healing. Heal me, God, heal me, Jesus!"

I sensed that the pastor was slowing down in his praying, so I prayed louder and louder. At the end, he stopped his prayer and invited those who received healing to the platform. I was extremely disappointed but I hid it and tried to be happy for those who were on the platform. I thought that since the service was not over, surely the pastor would pray one more time for those who could not receive healing and that God would heal me. As people were sharing their miraculous experiences and applauding amazing testimonies, the service came to an end without further prayer and healing. There was one more service in the morning and I thought to myself, "Tomorrow will be the day."

After the worship service I asked Sean how he felt. He said he was sorry to tell me that he no longer felt any discomfort in his hip or elbow. He'd been taking pain medication ever since his surgery, and even that evening he'd had some pain, but now it was gone. I told him that was awesome, but I said it bitterly. When I asked him why he kept backing up when the pastor shouted, he said he didn't know and that it was hard to explain. "I just felt something moving me." He went on to say that he didn't feel anything special in the moment, but now he felt so much peace and comfort in his body. "I am sorry," he said. "This is what you needed and wanted for a long time." I told him it was and that I was glad he felt good. I was sure I would receive healing the next morning. I hoped he had more faith in God after that experience. I was disappointed but thought that disappointment could be an obstacle to receive healing the next day. So I told God, "I still trust you. Please forgive my disappointment."

The next morning's service was held at a church near downtown Denver. Again, I got there early and was optimistic and hopeful. I had to be faithful regardless of what happened the previous night and what I had felt. Pastor Hinn prayed for people who were sick. I cried out to God for healing, but nothing was happening. With desperation and frustration, I wheeled down near the stage and cried out to God. Other people soon joined me in prayer. After ten minutes or so, he asked for the children of pastors to come up to the platform so he could pray for them. As people who were praying with me went back to their seats and PKs stepped up to the platform, I remained where I was near the platform.

There was a moment where the pastor and I made eye contact and the pastor signaled for one of his staff to bring me up to the platform. "Yes, praise God," I shouted, as there was no wheelchair ramp to the platform. I waited, but no one came. I reached out to one of the female staff and told her that the pastor wanted me to come up to the platform and asked her for help. She said, "He is just a man. Only God can heal you." I shouted, "Okay, okay. Please bring me to the platform." She said that she could not lift me. By this point the pastor had finished praying for the PKs and was about to conclude the service. I stared at him, hoping that he would see me and come down to the floor to lay his hands on me, but it never happened. The miracle crusades were over. Some people experienced healing, but many people remained in their wheelchairs.

It was tough to swallow the cup of bitterness and disappointment of that day. But I had to demonstrate to God that my faith was strong enough to receive healing. "Did Sean steal my thunder?" I wondered. "Did God make a mistake?" Why didn't anyone bring me up to the stage? If only I'd had faithful friends to lift me to the platform, like the friends who lowered the sickbed of their friend through a roof so he could be seen by Jesus. I wondered if that day would ever come for me. Then I told myself to stop doubting; it was the whisper of the devil. I was certain God was testing my faith, so I asked the Lord's forgiveness and told him that I trusted him and believed in him. "Please heal me in the name of Jesus Christ," I prayed. The day would come, and when it did, I would shout "This is my day!" But one way or another, that day was not my day.

Faith the Size of a Mustard Seed

Pastor Hinn taught that having faith the size of a mustard seed is the key to experiencing healing, supernatural events or miracles, and interpreting Jesus's teaching in Matt 17:20. After healing a demon-possessed boy who

Jesus's disciples could not heal, Jesus said, "Because you have so little faith. Truly I tell you, if you have faith as small as a mustard seed, you can say to this mountain, 'Move from here to there,' and it will move. Nothing will be impossible for you." I was fully convinced that all I needed was faith the size of the mustard seed to move my arms and legs again and go back to my former life. When I watched the Christian television programs, and saw people receiving miraculous healing from God and experiencing his supernatural power, I was excited and became passionate to pursue faith. However, growing my faith was difficult. I had been told that the fact that I could not move my body was evidence of my small faith and that having a strong faith in God required obeying his words. An obedient, repentant, and holy heart were the main ingredients to growing my faith. So I prayed, obeyed God's words, and repented of my transgressions. My time in praying, reading, and reflecting on the Bible—which used to be my favorite time of each day—was no longer a happy time and instead became a time of interrogating myself and searching for hidden and unrepented sins that I'd committed unconsciously and unintentionally. Things were not well within me, but I acted as if I was happy and grateful.

There were many times that I did feel happiness and gratitude, but as time passed and as my prayers for healing continued unanswered, my gratitude, joy, and peace soon faded into anxiety, doubt, and sorrow. I knew I could not dwell there for they were obstacles to growing my faith. So then I would repent of my anxiety, doubt, and sorrow and rebuke the devil out of me. The prosperity preachers on Christian television kept reminding me of the importance of strengthening my faith. I had to nurture it. Paul's teaching helped me to believe that I could reach the point where I could "do all things through him who gives me strength" (Phil 4:13). But I did not realize then that Paul's teaching was not about receiving everything we pray about or accomplishing everything that we put our mind to through the help of Jesus.

Back to School in 2006

I couldn't believe that I was reading a book on biology and preparing for an exam. After getting my GED in 2000 and dropping out of Arapahoe Community College in 2002, I was certain that I would never spend hours and hours reading, writing, and researching, let alone go back to college. As I started my journey with Jesus Christ, I sensed that God was stirring my heart to go back to school. I also knew that I had to do something to survive and live in this world. I knew that I needed more than a GED to begin a new career and find jobs that I could actually do because my physical disability limited me from performing many tasks.

But there weren't many options open to me. If I wasn't needed or wanted, what was the point of going back to school? Even with a diploma, I wasn't certain I could get a decent job or be needed by others. But maybe God could open new ways and train me. I was also hesitant to return to school because tuition was expensive for non-resident students like me. There were no government-funded scholarships or loan programs for us. Having no job, savings, scholarships, or money, I could not afford the tuition and could not ask my parents as they were already supporting me. But they encouraged me to start school and to search for more scholarships and grants. And even though it had been almost two years since I had been in contact with Lucy from Craig Hospital, my parents suggested contacting her as well. Despite feeling uncomfortable reaching out to her for help, after spending a few days in prayer, I gained enough confidence to email her for more information. She responded with a thoughtful and kind message and attached a file that contained many useful financial resources for people with disabilities.

Does God Know Our Needs?

I had to cross out many of the places in the file. As I had already failed to receive any grants or loans directly from the government, I crossed out the names of government-related organizations. And because of my undocumented immigration status, I crossed out organizations that offered support to residents and citizens of the US. What remained were a few nonprofit organizations that offered need-based scholarships and grants to people with disabilities. I was skeptical that they would actually approve my application because I was so used to receiving rejection letters. But to my surprise, I began receiving letters of acceptance.

They found my story heartbreaking but inspiring and were glad to support me with tuition. I also learned that I was qualified to receive funding because of my willingness and courage to go to school despite my physical and financial challenges. Instead of the sad and depressing message of "I am sorry, we cannot help you," I was hearing the exciting and joyful news of "Congratulations!" These expressions may have been out of simple courtesy, but I felt heard and accepted by them.

Many organizations were very generous in their financial support. I was able to start my journey of education through the generous donors of the Craig Alumni Scholarship Fund, which is dedicated to helping people with traumatic brain injuries and spinal cord injuries pursue education. I continued receiving their generous assistance over many years. The financial assistance from Joni & Friends helped me pay for tuition and repair my wheelchair. Kaiser offered a diversity scholarship twice to pay for tuition and educational expenses. There were also local organizations which helped me with my particular needs including medical supplies, dental work, and home modifications for my bathroom and desk. There was this indescribable satisfaction of doing things by myself again and of relieving some of the burden and responsibility of caregiving from Dad's shoulders.

In addition to the organizations from Lucy's list, other organizations also helped in many ways and at times that I was in the most need. It was as if they knew exactly what was happening in my personal life. God heard my prayers and had mercy on my family. He moved the hearts of people. While I was being overwhelmed by the kindness of the organizations, one nurse told me, "Surely you have a guiding angel watching over you." All of a sudden, with the help and assistance of all these various organizations, my lifestyle was upgraded. Although God did not give me healing, he strengthened me to believe in the power of prayer.

Making Sense of Prayers

Was there a guiding angel watching over me? Ever since God helped my family with the medical bills from Craig Hospital, many of my prayers were answered when I received grants, scholarships, and medical supplies. Did God use them to answer my prayers? Or were they simply wonderful organizations and individuals who were moved to help people in need like me? The main question I had was how much God was involved in moving them to make the decisions. These experiences could all be rationalized as the result of meeting the standards of the various programs; nothing more, nothing less. But if God moved their hearts, they would be a blessing for me.

Faith and skepticism collided in my thoughts. I wanted to believe they were acts of God, but I wondered if they were simply acts of people. Yet

God had to be involved because only he could answer my prayers and move their hearts. Only God could actually heal me. If he could not even answer these types of prayers, how could he supernaturally heal my spinal cord injury?

I finally had to acknowledge these provisions as God's answers to my prayers because they continued happening and because of the degree of confidence and conviction that filled my heart. Thanking God became natural and comfortable without doubt or awkwardness. My prayers of gratitude no longer felt like lip service to God. They were authentic words from deep inside me. I no longer questioned God's existence; his mercy and compassion became ever more real to me. Without feeling doubt or resistance within me, I could confess that God hears our prayers and answers them in his power. It was like my relationship with God entered a higher level, as if my faith leveled up.

For a long time my faith had depended on the experiences and faith of my parents and others. Their stories of God's compassion and answered prayers became my stories of the God of the Bible and the testimony of my God. The God of Abraham, Isaac, and Jacob was also my Provider and God. This was a good sign that I was going in the right direction and that the day of healing was coming soon. Yes, I was filled with optimism, hope, and faith and could feel them in the air.

Enjoying My Studies

School was not too bad. Actually, aside from taking exams, the other requirements—reading books on different subjects, reflecting on different concepts and systems of thought, and writing papers—were manageable and even enjoyable. I could finish all my core courses online; the online educational platform was perfect for me. Online interaction was my only social interaction with people because I did not have many occasions for outside activities and meetings. It surely was a special time.

A school counselor told me about the Americans with Disabilities Act (ADA) and its effort to help students with disabilities succeed in academic settings and accommodate their needs. According to the ADA, all educational institutions in America are legally obligated to offer accommodation to all medically qualified and approved students with certain physical or psychological conditions or disabilities. Accommodations can include providing extra time to complete assignments and exams, offering a private space to take exams without distractions, helping with taking notes in the classroom, taking exams in a private room, and finding electronic resources for required course textbooks. When electronic resources were not available, they scanned my books and provided them in electronic formats. These are examples of the accommodation that I received, and they were very helpful for my studies.

Challenges

With my physical challenges, studying was not always easy. The first challenge was the speed of my typing. Because of my injury level, I could move my arms and wrists and elbows, but not my fingers, so I had to put typing sticks on my hands to type and use the computer. Occupational therapists from Craig Hospital told me about Dragon, a voice recognition program that helps people operate a computer and type by using their voices. Dragon, at least for me, was great for writing journal and personal reflection papers, but it was not accurate enough for academic papers. So I typed all my academic and important papers and used the Dragon software for free writing and reflection papers.

At first I complained about my slow typing speed and using the mouse pad with my limited hand movement. Typing was tiring and I grew weary after two hours or so until I became stronger and could type for many hours a day. Because of the number of hours I typed and my body posture in my wheelchair, neck and shoulder pain became a normal part of daily life. Having insufficient body movement for appropriate stretching and exercise and receiving therapies intensified the muscle pain over the years.

The second challenge was nerve pain in my thigh area. It felt like a burning sensation and was not manageable. Although I tried to adjust my body posture, it was almost impossible. Tilting my wheelchair often helped, but I could not stay in that position all day long. I had occasionally felt the pain after I was discharged from the hospital, but it continued to grow. Later, when I had health insurance, my primary doctor prescribed medication which made me too drowsy to concentrate on my research and work. There were many times when I could not even pray to God because of the level of the nerve pain. Therefore, I had to suck it up and depend on God for his help and comfort, praying more than I had committed to do and relying on him for all my needs.

The third challenge was tilting my wheelchair every fifteen to twenty minutes for five minutes. I considered it a waste of time and complained to God, but I felt I had no choice because shifting my weight was the only way to prevent pressure sores. Taking these five-minute breaks broke the rhythm of whatever activity I was engaging in and I often forgot what I had been reading and thinking about. When I tilted my chair, I often lost track of the time and fell into daydreaming. I hated this time of tilting. But God gradually gave me many ideas of things to do during the five minutes such as praying, reciting Bible verses, singing a song, and meditation. The meaningless five minutes became meaningful and precious. President Abraham Lincoln supposedly once said, "If I only had an hour to chop down a tree, I would spend the first forty-five minutes sharpening my axe." For me, these five minutes became a time for sharpening an axe to chop more trees.

Another challenge was that at school, unlike at home, I felt embarrassed about being in a wheelchair. The classroom experience was somewhat complicated. I wished I didn't need to ask others for help, but I couldn't open or close doors by myself and needed classmates to move desks to make space for me. I often had to park my wheelchair at the front of classrooms and was frequently close to the professors' desks. And although I did not want to do it, especially in small classrooms, I had to tilt my wheelchair; I had no choice, otherwise I would pay a high price.

I knew that my classmates and professors didn't care too much about me and wouldn't make fun of me or bully me, but humiliation and shame filled my heart. I was embarrassed because I had not been like this before the snowboarding accident. I used to be confident, whether it was due to the influence of cocaine or the result of the approval from my coworkers. It could have been having clear dreams and high confidence that I would be successful and accomplish them. After the accident I became a completely different person and had to apply a new perspective to my thinking because my old way of thinking caused insecurity and low self-esteem.

American history, held in a big lecture hall, became my favorite class. The lecture hall had four wide entrances and spacious aisles between seats and rows. Because of its size, there were still many empty seats along the sides. I was therefore able to enter the lecture hall, find an empty space on the farthest side where I could tilt my wheelchair without feeling embarrassed, and even exit the hall independently. I wished I could meet fellow students in wheelchairs with more experience to strengthen my weak mentality. But I had always been the only person in a wheelchair at the school.

I was one of a kind. When I thought of it that way, it did not feel too bad. I was special and unique.

The last challenge was dealing with pressure sores. The first pressure sore happened in 2008 while I was an undergraduate student. At first, Dad thought that it looked like rash. After about a week, the rash became a small wound so we decided to go to the CICP clinic so I could be seen by its medical team. After examining the sore, they gave me a few patches to cover the sore and instructed me on how to use them to take care of it. But after a month, it was bigger and uglier. Later, I found out that the nurses at the clinic were not wound specialists. Because I did not have health insurance, I called Lucy and explained to her about the wound and my financial situation. She helped me get seen by the nurses who specialize in treating pressure sores at Craig Hospital.

When the nurses examined my wound, they determined that I must take a more proactive approach to heal the pressure sore because of its severity. Fortunately it was not severe enough to infect my hip bone. They cleaned it and attached an antibiotic patch on it. I thought that the treatment was over and that the sore would heal right away. When I asked them what I needed to do, they told me to tilt my wheelchair every fifteen minutes and stay in bed for twenty hours a day so that I would not add more pressure to the sore. At first I thought the nurse was overreacting. How could I stay in bed twenty hours a day?

After my visit at Craig Hospital, I tried to tilt more often and to spend more time in bed to take the pressure off my thigh. After a month, I met with the wound specialists again to check on the progress of healing, and they told me that the sore was not getting better. In fact, despite my extra effort and prayer, it was getting worse. They asked me if I had followed their instructions, and I told them that I did the tilting and stayed in bed longer, but not for twenty hours a day. It was not enough. They said that if I did not stay in bed for twenty hours a day for the next two or three months, my sore would not heal. It was my only option unless I was willing to have surgery.

For the next three months, my lifestyle changed completely. After Dad transferred me to my wheelchair at 9:00 in the morning, I washed my face and hands, ate breakfast, checked my email, worked on coursework, and prepared to do things in bed. I took fewer showers; I was not going anywhere. Thinking that every fifteen minutes was not good enough, I never forgot to recline my wheelchair every thirteen minutes for five minutes. While reclined, I thought about the things that I was supposed to execute for the next fourteen minutes. Once the clock hit the five-minute mark, I was back up to execute the tasks. After being up for three hours, Dad transferred me back to my bed around noon.

My hospital bed could elevate the upper part of the bed but not high enough for me to sit up. I could not read or eat on the bed. Dad had to feed me lunch and dinner one bite at a time. I had done that before when I was at Craig, so it was not so bad, but eating took a good twenty to thirty minutes because I had to chew and swallow slowly to avoid food going down the wrong pipe. After lunch, I read books for two hours or so until my arms were too tired to hold papers. Dad would copy thirty to fifty pages of a book and lay them next to my head. I held one page at a time, read it, dropped it on the floor, got the next page from my side, read it, dropped it, and so forth. Having incomplete movement in my arms, I held the paper by putting the right side of the paper between my right index and middle finger and doing the same for the other side. Holding pages wore down my arms very quickly. After two hours of reading, I was done. I tried to find a better way to read longer and more easily. Many options that I found on the internet were not suitable for my situation. I tried audio books many times but fell asleep often. Kindle was too heavy and small to hold with my two hands, and there was no other way to read books. Besides, between 2008 and 2013, even though my school offered online courses, there were no recorded lectures for my classes, so reading and studying in bed was the only way to take my courses.

I begged for God to heal the pressure sore and have mercy on me. The days in bed were long. I prayed that the wound would be healed as quickly as possible and hoped that Dad would say the sore was healed when he examined it each morning. I used to think my wheelchair was a torture chair, but when I saw it next to my bed, I thought, "Oh, I wish to be in my wheelchair."

Why Me? Why Not Me?

For the first few weeks of the bed care, I could endure the change, discomfort, and frustration; however, after the first month passed by, I became impatient and agitated physically and spiritually. I tried to be positive in the presence of my parents because they were also having a difficult time seeing me in bed all day long and were also going through hell. I tried to be faithful to God, thinking that God would not help the speed of the recovery if

I complained to him. However, my patience and faith reached their limits, and I could not hold back my disappointment and frustration any longer and cried out to God. "Why God, why me? I never asked you this when I had the accident because I knew I was not in a position to ask you the question. But, Lord, I have been faithful to you for the last four years."

I went on to detail the ways in which I had been faithful: I read the Bible, memorized Bible verses, prayed, and thanked him even when I did not feel like it. I quit my worldly habits, stopped watching sexual and immoral content to resist any temptations, and tried to do everything I could to obey and please him. It had only been four years, but I was still suffering through all of these challenges. Had not my parents and I cried a river? If God knew the degree of my suffering, why wasn't he healing me miraculously? Why did I have to suffer so much? I told him it wasn't fair. Was it naïve of me to think that my situation was unfair? After all, we all live in an unfair world corrupted by immorality, pride, selfishness, greed, lies, and hatred. What was a fair amount of hardship that should be on my plate? How much suffering was enough?

Then again, why not me? Was I somehow more special than other people that I shouldn't have to suffer the pain of the SCI and pressure sore? But at the very least, the pressure sore was too much on top of my paralysis struggles. How was I supposed to interpret the meaning, cause, and purpose of the pressure sore and its terrible implications on my family's life and mine when I could not resolve the issues with God about my spinal cord injury?

I did not have answers to these questions. I wanted to explore them further, but I felt uncomfortable even with the idea of having a conversation with God. It seemed inappropriate somehow. How can a creature argue with his or her God? Once again, I felt fear over questioning God and of irritating him to the point where he would not heal me. At first I wanted to know the answers and felt like the main character of a movie who is searching for the truth at all costs. Gradually I wondered, "What if I knew the truth? What would the truth change about my situation? Would it heal me? Would it satisfy me? And what if I did not like the answer?"

I could not do anything else to speed up the process of healing the sore so I focused on the present and my responsibility. As a student, I was responsible for completing course assignments, reading required texts, memorizing important concepts, and writing papers. As a believer, my responsibilities were to obey my Lord and Savior, praise him for my salvation, pray, meditate on his words, and thank him not only for the opportunity to study regardless of my disability, but also for the treatment at Craig Hospital and its wonderful nurses and my loving parents, understanding that many people who have spinal cord injuries in other countries do not have a suitable environment in which to take care of their wounds. I was filled with uncertainty and anxiety deep inside my heart, but I did try to do my best to be grateful.

As my pressure sore healed, my spirit regained its strength, joy, and gratitude. After almost four months, the pressure sore was finally healed and was covered with new skin. The nurses recommended adding hours back in the wheelchair over time and once again warned me of the danger of the recurrence of a pressure sore. So I followed their instructions and committed to do the weight shifting religiously.

Unfortunately, that was not the last episode of having a pressure sore. Despite my best efforts, I had six episodes of pressure sores between 2008 and 2013. My daily routine was to start my day in my wheelchair at 9:00 in the morning and be transferred to my bed at 5:00 every evening for five years except when the pressure sore needed an extra treatment. Whenever Dad observed a red spot on the scar of the pressure sore, I was transferred to bed earlier in the day, at 3:00 in the afternoon or perhaps at 1:00, depending on the condition of the sore. A few times I was bedbound for twenty hours a day for few weeks at a time like I was the first time.

Between 2008 and 2013, reading and studying in bed was the only way to take my online courses during both my undergraduate and graduate studies. Consequently, when I attended in-person classes, my priority always had been going to class and leaving right away to go home and get ready to study in bed. Thus, building and having fellowship with classmates and professors was a luxury that I could not afford in order to protect my skin and to live life again. Truly, my life was not normal and did not make any sense.

Thankfully, I graduated from Iliff School of Theology in 2013 but had to stay in bed for two months the summer before starting the fall semester at Denver Seminary. The solution was always simple: the more I stayed in bed the faster the wound healed. By some miracle, once I began my studies at Denver Seminary, I stopped getting pressure sores. Nothing had changed. Did God pay special attention to my desperate and sincere prayers? Seeing that my skin was getting healthier without any issues, I gradually spent more time in the wheelchair and had dinner at the table with my family.

In 2014, I transferred to my bed at 7:00 in the evening, and by the time I graduated from Denver Seminary in 2016, I was healthy enough to be up until 9:00. This was a very good life. Still, I had to do the weight shifting religiously and pay careful attention to the scar because it could erupt anytime that it was not managed appropriately. For this reason, unlike other students, I could not afford to stay up late at night.

Light Rail

After completing all my core courses at Arapahoe Community College in 2008, I decided to transfer to the University of Colorado, Denver, a four-year university located in downtown Denver. I used Denver Light Rail to attend classes because courses for my major were not offered online at ACC. Dad dropped me off at the light rail station and I would wait on a special platform constructed for those who needed help with access to the light rail train. When a train arrived, an operator would drop down a ramp that connected the outside platform to the train entrance, and I would wheel into the train and park at the handicapped seating near the door. The ride was not the most comfortable or pleasant, but I enjoyed it very much. I was able to look outside and see people interacting in real life, and I tasted the sweetness of freedom and independence inside the train for thirty minutes. Was it human nature that desired freedom and independence, or was it just me?

After getting out at the campus I would see students hanging around with their friends. Sometimes they were sitting or lying on the grass, smoking cigarettes, or playing guitar and cards. They looked so free, doing what they wanted to do by moving their hands, feet, and bodies. Actually, I was happy that I could also be outside by myself, wheel around the campus, and be independent. But as soon as I saw people doing what I wanted to do, I fell into the trap of feeling embarrassed and sorry for myself, and complaining about what I did not have. "No, don't go there," I would think, and rush to my classroom.

"I Am with You"

One day, as I was wheeling to the light rail station, I saw students who looked very happy and free hanging out with their friends. By comparison, I looked lonely and miserable. All of a sudden I thought, "What if LeBron James, BTS, and Jeff Bezos were my friends and were with me at this very moment? Would I still feel depressed and ashamed of myself? Wouldn't those students come to me and want to be my friend to get to know them? Would I still feel insecure about not having a job and money? No, I would be very confident and feel so secure that I would hold my head high." And, that is when this small, calm voice spoke to my heart: "the one who is greater than LeBron James or Bill Gates is with you. The one who is more powerful than any president or ruler of this world is with you. The one who has all the wealth and riches in this universe is with you. The one who loves you more than your friends and parents is with you. The one who suffered and died for your transgressions is with you. I am with you."

In that moment, everything changed. I had been so focused on myself that my condition defined the degree and quality of my confidence and self-esteem. I had nothing to boast about myself. As a child of God, however, my glorious identity in him was defined by who God is and what he had done for me on the cross. The more I shifted my attention to him, the more I gained confidence and strength; God became my confidence.

Say the Magic Words

As I studied and read the Bible, I became more compelled to believe that God has the power to heal all sickness, including my spinal cord injury. I wasn't sure when the day of healing would come, but it had to come. My journey with Jesus was not perfect, but I tried to do everything to obey God's words and believe in him and distance myself from a worldly lifestyle. I constantly examined my faith and mind to make sure that they had no doubt or error. If I found any sinful thought, I repented of my sin right away. Constantly interrogating myself and pointing out my guilt as a sinner was modern-day self-flagellation. I abused myself and whipped my spirit because doubt would be counted as unbelief and discredit my faith in God. This type of practice and mindset continued for years and became my lifestyle.

Everything I did was out of motivation to receive healing from God, so I had a daily prayer regimen. First I confessed God's power and love. Then I asked God Almighty to heal my spinal cord injury. After that I asked the God of love to have mercy on me, just as a blind man asked Jesus to have mercy on him and received his sight. Finally, I reminded God of his words and promises. I would recite biblical passages and stories related to God's healing. For example, I prayed, "Lord Jesus, in Matthew 7:7 you told us to ask and we would receive. Even though doctors cannot heal me, I believe that you can heal me. I ask for healing. Please heal me according to your promises. I am simply obeying your words."

Still nothing happened. I was still in a wheelchair. After all these years of asking for God's healing, my body was still stiff. In the Gospel of John, there was a man who could not walk for thirty-eight years but received healing when Jesus told him to pick up his mat and walk (John 5:8). I wondered if I would have to wait thirty years for Jesus to tell me to get up out of my wheelchair and walk. Jesus told his disciples, "If you remain in me and my words remain in you, ask whatever you wish, and it will be done for you" (John 15:7). I wondered if I had to memorize more Scripture. How many words had to remain in me? One hundred words? One thousand words? In other instances Jesus simply healed people who were sick because he had compassion on them. Was my suffering not severe enough for God to show compassion to me? Would I have to suffer more to get his attention and cry out louder until I lost my voice? Why was he not healing me? I was doing everything I could to obey him. I tried to be thankful even when I didn't feel like it. I praised him while my heart felt sorrow. I held on to his words and promises, wondering what else I must do to strengthen my faith.

My Breakthrough

I began reflecting on my unanswered prayers theologically. I wondered why God wouldn't heal me if he were all powerful, all loving, and all merciful. Had God's power decreased since the time of the Bible? If so, he would not have been able to heal people like he did during Pastor Hinn's miracle crusades or other televised Christian programs. Nor could he save sinners and come again to judge the world on the last day. If he were not all powerful, everything would fall apart, even my salvation and eternal life. I did not want to consider this. The sermons of those televangelists echoed in my mind when I wanted to reason with God. I remembered phrases such as "Jesus is a healer. He wants to heal you. Jesus always wants to do more miracles, but your lack of faith prevents him from doing more in your lives," and corresponding passages such as Matt 13:58.

I also recalled them saying that we did not have what we asked for because our faith was too weak. God promised that he would answer the prayer of the faithful, so we were to keep cultivating and training our faith through continuous and sincere obedience. I could not reason against what seemed to be biblically and theologically correct teaching. If there was nothing wrong with the teaching, especially the theological aspect of God's power and healing, the issue had to be me. My small faith must be insufficient to move him to heal me. Even questioning God would be sinful and damage my faith, so I must repent of my sin. God could not be too weak to heal me and could not be wrong; otherwise, everything that I had already sacrificed would be meaningless and my effort for nothing. I had come too far to turn my back against him at that moment.

As I reflected on these challenges, all of a sudden I heard God asking me questions in my heart. The first was, "Will you still love me even if I do not heal you?" I tried to ignore it, but again I heard, "Will you still read the Bible even if I do not heal you? Will you still memorize Bible verses?" I was certain that this was the voice of Satan. I did not think my good, loving, and almighty God would ask such absurd questions. Of course God will heal me. It was not a question of whether he would heal me but when. He could, he should, and he must, right? These questions lingered in my heart for days and weeks and became louder and clearer. God was asking me questions. He demanded my response.

I could not and did not want to answer the questions. I needed and wanted healing from him to start a new life. I had made my own plans for God to use me as an evangelist to share about his miraculous power with the world and to send me around the world to unknown places to tell believers and nonbelievers that God is still alive and still works wonders. I wanted God to accomplish these plans, and healing was necessary. But now he was telling me that my plan was not his plan for me. At the same time, God's questions were his response to the prayers that I had been praying for a long time. That was the moment when he actually answered my prayer, but I never imagined that he would respond to my prayers by asking questions that I did not want to and could not answer.

Did I want to move my legs and hands? Yes! Did I want to take a walk outside with my parents and dog? Did I want to get up by myself, take a shower, make my bed, and start my daily life? Yes. I did not want anything fancy. I just wanted to be normal and do what other people do. If I didn't receive healing, I did not know how I could take care of myself. I did not know how God expected me to live with no movement in my arms and legs. I wanted to care for my parents when they were older. I had many reasons for receiving healing from God. Still, God was asking me to give up what I had been begging of him for many years and what I treasured the most. The final questions boiled down to this: Did I want healing more than God? Would I choose God or healing? Could I choose God over healing?

Let Me Be Your Hands and Feet

One morning when I was reading the Bible and praying about those questions, something was different. Something was happening to me. My heart was pounding and even squeezing my chest, and I felt my blood pressure and temperature going up. I felt tense and a tingling sensation all over my body. I had never had a heart attack, but maybe this was one. In that tense moment, God asked me the questions again. I was scared to live with a disability and I could not let go of my dream of walking again. But God gave me a verse: "'For I know the plans I have for you,' declares the Lord, 'plans to prosper you and not to harm you, plans to give you hope and a future'" (Jer 29:11). Gently, God spoke to my heart: "Let me be your legs and hands." At that moment I felt and received enough strength and confidence from the Spirit to confess in words, "Lord, I want to walk again. I still believe you can heal me. You gave me your Son Jesus Christ, and I give you this broken body. Doctors told me that I would never walk again, but I will follow you for the rest of my life even if you don't heal me. Please take care of me and my family."

Right after that confession, the discomfort, pressure, and tension were gone. My heart melted. It felt as though so much weight had been thrown off my body. I had never felt so much tranquility in my life. Tears flowed down my face. When I opened my eyes, I thought I would go through an additional supernatural or transcendent experience and that I would receive a gift of prophecy or healing. None of that happened at that time. However, there was freedom, freedom from the need to receive healing and to have specific prayers answered.

Freedom

Since that day, God has slowly enlightened my eyes to see that Pastor Hinn's teaching about faith and receiving healing was unbiblical. I fell into the trap of thinking that my faith was the means to receive what I wanted from God. I was so focused on receiving what I wanted that my relationship with him became focused on his healing and powerful hands, and neglected to seek his face. I called out to God for miracles, but muted his voice and plan. I mistook God for a genie in a lamp, thinking that if I rubbed the lamp hard and long enough, he would come out and grant my wishes. In my prayers I said that God was my Lord, but in reality acted as if I was the Lord and could demand that he give me what I wanted. If he didn't, I was almost ready to deny his existence and walk away from him. Perhaps I took Jesus as a hostage and tried to negotiate with the Holy Spirit to demand my reward from the Father through his words and promises. If God did not grant me my needs and prayers, he could not be a good and loving God. I put myself above God and my desires above his. My desires became a god that I worshipped. Both God and faith were the means to walking again.

It was around this time that I finally understood and accepted that the purpose of my life was to glorify God, which was the evolution of discovering God's new dream for me. I read Pastor Rick Warren's book, *The Purpose Driven Life*, a book that teaches that the purpose of human beings is to glorify God. However, its teaching somehow did not sink within me when I read it during the first year of my new life. I guess I was so worked up about receiving healing from God that I could not accept or embrace any wisdom unrelated to receiving healing from God. This understanding was confirmed gradually through God's teaching in 1 Corinthians: "So whether you eat or drink or whatever you do, do it all for the glory of God" (1 Cor 10:31). Therefore, I had to live my life for the glory of God, regardless of my circumstances and unfulfilled desires. It was for this very relationship with God that I was created as a human being on this earth. Circumstances should not change the purpose of my life, and whether I had a disability or not, I needed to glorify God. As his adopted child in Jesus, I needed to love God and love others as Jesus loved me.

Although I want to walk again, I finally understood that I did not have to walk again in order to accomplish his purpose for my life. I can freely choose not to walk again if God has special plans to be glorified through me in a wheelchair. I can choose to please God and not myself because he is the Lord of every part of my life. And I can still freely choose God, his grace over my healing, his dreams over my plans, and his glory over my pleasures. Even if I could walk again, it would be to glorify God; therefore, whether I could move or not, all I had to do was wheel after him. Strong and mature faith is admirable, but it is for God's glory, not for receiving something from God. Finally, I was free to live.

My desire for healing has not changed, neither has my belief that God is Almighty to heal me. I still want to be able to massage the shoulders and arms of my parents, cook for them, run their errands, pick up their medication and groceries, and return what they have sacrificed for me. I want to repay what God, my parents, wonderful friends, organizations, and other people have done for me. What has changed is that my love for and faith in Jesus no longer depends on my circumstances and conditions. I can love God even if he does not heal me. I can believe that Jesus is my Lord and Savior even if I cannot move my hands and feet. I can still follow him in my wheelchair because what I already have in and received from God is much greater than the healing that I want and the suffering that I experience every moment and every day. My relationship with God is greater than my prosperity, happiness, and health, although I may pray for them and complain to him about not having them.

My love for God, of course, is far from perfect for it fluctuates in all directions when the wind blows; however, I know that despite the levels of the wind, God will hold me with his righteous right hand, strengthen me with his mighty hands, and comfort me with his nail-pierced hands. I am wheeling with Jesus and will wheel with him for the rest of my life. I will eventually walk with him eternally. If suffering with a disability shall be part of my journey with Jesus, I will bear it as my cross and follow him, for he will bear it with me.

Two Lumps

In early 2009, after recovering from the pain of enduring the three months of treating the pressure sore in 2008, I began having fever-like symptoms. During the days I felt so cold that I put on thick sweaters and jackets, constantly drank hot water, and put hot packs on my shoulders. At nights, I turned on the electric bed sheet and put on a thick blanket. I shivered for at least two hours until I became so overheated that I needed to take away the thick blanket, drink ice-cold water, and put a cold washcloth on my body to bring my temperature down.

For some reason, at first, neither my parents nor I considered these to be serious changes. What could they possibly mean? What more could happen after the ordeal with the pressure sores? However, after five days, the symptoms worsened, and I had sharp pain when I swallowed food. Although I knew that something was definitely wrong, I did not want to go to the hospital because of the cost of medical treatment. I just prayed to God for his direct intervention and healing. After having a fever for two weeks and not having enough sleep at night, I was tired and sick but was still too stubborn to go to the hospital.

About the third week, Dad felt something unusual behind my back and asked me if it hurt when he pushed on it. I didn't feel anything. He told me that there were two lumps the size of a small fist on my spine. He insisted we go to the hospital. I went back to Craig Hospital and thought that solving the problem would be as easy as removing fluid or some other procedure that wouldn't be so expensive. The outpatient nurses at Craig Hospital examined my lumps and determined that I needed to go to the emergency room right away. I couldn't understand why they were overreacting to those lumps. The emergency staff thought that I had tuberculosis and isolated me in a separate room. As they put a special gown on me and gave one to Dad, fear fell upon me.

Get Me Out!

After drawing my blood and getting a urine sample to figure out the cause of the infection and lumps, they put me in a narrow dark tube to run an MRI. I didn't have any phobia, but the thirty minutes in the tube was like going through hell. Having drunk so much water, my bladder was full and reached its capacity. Then, the pounding headache, severe pain in my body, and rising body temperature hit me like a tsunami. I knew that I was having hyperreflexia. I pushed the button inside the MRI tube to talk to the technician, but there was no response. I pushed it again and again. Nothing happened. I screamed for help, but the MRI was too loud and swallowed my desperate screaming. The tube was dark and so narrow that I could not even move my arms. I could feel my blood pressure getting higher as my pounding headache and body pain increased, and I thought that I would have a stroke and die in the tube. When fear and frustration hit me, I could not breath and I was certain that the MRI tube was about to become my coffin.

At that moment, God moved in my heart and reminded me that this was not the end and could not be the end. I began taking deep breaths and calmed myself down, asking God for his help. Slowly, I was able to endure the pain and fear for a few minutes. Thankfully, the technician eventually asked me how I was doing and pulled me out right away. (I do not recall clearly, but I may have poured out words of criticisms and curses.) Still, the doctors could not find the problem. Only after running a CAT scan they found something wrong with my neck. I was hospitalized that night and I worried about the cause of the problem as well as certain medical expenses. My body felt like it was burning all night, but in order to be ready for a possible surgery, I could not drink any water.

Swedish Hospital

The next morning, a team of doctors visited me and explained what was happening to my body. The CAT scan showed that there was a hole in my esophagus; pieces of food and water that I swallowed went into the hole and caused big lumps on both sides of my back. Consequently, various types of bacteria grew in the lumps, feasting on the pieces of food and water. Therefore, infection caused the fever, but fortunately the bacteria that grew in the lumps did not infect other organs. The bacteria and infection needed to be treated to avoid the worst scenario. Three surgeries had to occur in one setting. First, one surgeon made insertions behind my back near the lumps to drain the nasty fluid and clean up the lumps and other areas near them. He put extra tubes in them to get additional fluid that could not be drained completely. Another surgeon performed the same procedure of cleaning the front of my neck. The other surgeon made another insertion in front of my neck and closed the torn esophagus by grafting a piece of joint from my hip. The surgery took almost twelve hours.

When I opened my eyes, I saw my parents and medical team. The surgeon who was in charge of the surgery told me that the surgery went well and that my esophagus had been torn by a metal plate that was inserted on my spinal cord when I had the spinal cord fusion surgery after my snowboarding accident. It was supposed to be removed after a few years, but I don't recall anyone telling me about that. According to the doctor, this type of problem was not uncommon. In order to be discharged from the hospital, the infection and fever had to stop and the hole must be completely healed. I was on twelve types of antibiotics because the doctors couldn't figure out the exact bacteria that was causing the infection and fever. To heal the hole, the surgical area on my esophagus had to be dried without any contact with food. I was ordered not to drink any liquid or eat anything. At first I received nutrients through a tube inserted in my nose. Having no strength, I ended up lying in bed all day. As my stay at the hospital continued, a doctor inserted a feeding tube into my stomach for more nutrients. So, four years after the DVT surgery, I was hospitalized again.

More Misery?

Hoping to go home in a week, I made a daily plan to live a productive and spiritual hospital life. I woke up at 7:00 in the morning to start my day just like I did at home. That's when the morning shift began, and nurses and tech checked my vitals and helped me wash my face and brush my teeth. After that, I did my morning devotions which included watching a Christian television program, prayer, and meditating on Bible verses. Next, I called my parents to tell them that I was doing okay so that they would not come to the hospital to check up on me. The morning routine took two to three hours. Since I couldn't be in a wheelchair or use a computer, I didn't have much to do after that. I prayed three times a day, and James called me every day from California after work while he was stuck in traffic. We usually talked about eating. Or rather I talked about how I was not able to eat anything, not even clear liquid for the first two months or so. I was going crazy.

I had daily visits from the medical team: Dr. Gof, internal medicine doctors, their interns, lab technicians who drew my blood at least three times a week, respiratory technicians who brought inhalers to break up mucus from my lungs, nurses, techs, and my parents. Still, I had plenty of time and felt guilty for wasting time in the hospital and worrying about hospital bills. After one month, Dr. Gof wrote an order for clear liquid such as water, apple juice, certain Gatorades, and Jell-O. I never knew until that day that drinking water could taste so sweet and that I enjoyed eating Jell-O so much. As the sweetness of the cold Jell-O melted on my tongue, the dark world looked brighter and more optimistic.

C. diff

Another humiliation happened in that hospital room. Because of the antibiotics and staying at the hospital for more than two months, I had this nasty diarrhea disease called C. diff. Being confined to the hospital bed, I could not control it. One night I had diarrhea on the bed and the tech cleaned after me. As soon as he was done cleaning up and moved my body to one side of the bed to put on a clean bed sheet, I had another episode. I felt so much humiliation and apologized over not having any control. By the seventh episode, I had lost my dignity and had no words to express how sorry I was. As he walked out of the room, tears flowed down my face. I felt terrible for him and humiliated over my inability to clean up after myself. This repeated sense of helplessness led to desperation and anxiety. If I could not even do that, I wondered how I could survive in the world.

Another Testing Ground

Being hospitalized at Swedish, I was getting sick and tired of being sick and tired. The time when I'd been at home doing bed care for the pressure sore was a luxury compared to this. There I was able to use the computer, eat whatever I wanted, drink as much as I could, do many indoor and outdoor activities in my wheelchair, and take showers. But I could not do anything in the hospital bed. This time I lay in bed twenty-four hours a day, shivering all day and night with body aches. The uncertainty of not knowing the exact bacteria that was causing the infection and fever even after the surgery caused tension and even fear. I was getting tired of hospital life. Having people knocking on the door to draw blood in the middle of the night when I finally was about to fall asleep became annoying. And there were a few new lab technicians who had no clue what they were doing. Even though I had an IV, fresh blood had to be drawn from other parts of my body for accurate results. I suffered with the constant humiliation of wetting my hospital bed and feeling sorry for the nurses and techs, and not understanding why I was going through this challenge.

Dr. Gof could not assure me how long it would take for the tear to be healed completely and mentioned that it could take a week or ten weeks. I always focused on one week. I knew that I could wait for one week, but not for three weeks. The condition of the tear on my esophagus was inspected through an X-ray every Monday morning and it became the most exciting day of the week. If there was a leak, that meant more hospitalization; without a leak, it meant I could finally go home. I always prayed that it would be the day of praise for my miraculous healing. To examine whether there was a leak on my esophagus, I had to swallow a dark, bitter solution. I had to wait until the afternoon to find out the results. For almost two months I heard the same answer: there was still a leak in my esophagus. Those Monday afternoons were frustrating and disappointing. My hope for a miracle began fading away like a mirage.

Once again I was thrown into a place of doubt and wondered whether all the things that I had experienced since my accident were simply the outcome of natural human events rather than supernatural events initiated by God. If God was never part of the experiences that I considered to be his miraculous and direct work, what had I been believing? Had I been blinded to the truth because of my needs and desperation? Was my faith blind? Did I make up my own experiences as defense mechanism? Did I believe that God adds meaning to what's meaninglessness, hope to hopelessness, or purpose to an aimless life? Was Karl Marx right when he said that religion was the opiate of the people? What about the freedom that I felt that day? What about the words that God spoke to my heart? Was I daydreaming again?

I began to investigate everything that I believed, confessed, and experienced. It was an investigation of God, and I asked him to respond to my accusations. "Answer me, Lord. Answer me, for I need your response. How can a good and moral God allow me to go through this horrible situation? How can a God who foreknows all things still allow me to be confined to this bed? Why didn't you prevent the tear that made a hole in my neck?" No one in the hospital knew that I was wrestling with God. No one knew why I would put the blankets over me or why I turned up the volume of the television to scream my lungs out in the endless cycle of shivering.

Isaiah 41:10

One night when I prayed to him, God answered me through his words in Isa 41:10: "So do not fear, for I am with you; do not be dismayed, for I am your God. I will strengthen you and help you; I will uphold you with my righteous right hand." I had already memorized the verse and used to think that it had a good and comforting tone. It did not make much impact on my life. But it was at that moment that I realized God was with me. He was at the side of my bed, in the very room where I was bedbound. He convinced me that the God to whom I was calling from under the bedsheet was the Lord of hosts who is in control of all affairs, foreknows all future events and human choices, and is mighty to save me from the current situation.

His words demolished the stronghold of my doubt. It was torn down like the wall of Jericho. Surely what I wanted from God was a miraculous breakthrough. I believed God was able to bring forth such an event. I did not actually want to be comforted in my heart and strengthened in my faith. All I wanted was healing. However, the confirmation that God was with me and the promise that he would strengthen me, help me, and uphold me with this righteous right hand was more pleasing, powerful, and moving in my heart than the very healing for which I had been praying. Amazingly, his words and promises were more than enough for me and calmed the storm in me. Physical healing had not come, but he strengthened me to trust in his goodness and love and affirmed that I was already held by his mighty hands and that he would always hold me, even if I let go. I was fully convinced that he would scoop me out of the room and plant me by the streams of water. So much peace filled my heart. I wanted to be out of the hospital but I was content and satisfied in his words and promises that were moving and active within me. For me, this was a miracle. Maybe this was the miracle that my spirit needed in order to be healthier and stronger to trust in God.

Grace

Gratitude filled my heart. I was grateful that I was being treated in such a wonderful facility with such good doctors, nurses, and techs. I was grateful for the tech who took care of my mess. I was grateful for those who cleaned my room, drew my blood, and transported me to the X-ray rooms. I was grateful for the friend who called me every day and my parents and friends who visited me. I was grateful for the renewed conviction that it was God who had orchestrated all the help I'd received from people and organizations. I was grateful for God.

Yes, I prayed to God, and he responded to my prayer in ways that I did not expect. Still, I could not understand why he was so good to me. Why does this God Almighty, the holy and righteous One, choose to have mercy on me, an unfaithful, complaining, and ungrateful sinner? Why should he answer my prayers? Why is he with me? Why does he choose to stay with me when I've filled this room with grumbling? It's not like I have done enough deeds to gain his favor. Is it because he loves me? If so, why does he love me? Why does he keep telling me that he loves me? He does not have to love me. I did not do anything to move him to love me. I defamed him before the accident. I told people around me that I was a Christian while drinking and doing drugs. A few of them thought that I was like a devil. I do not love God that much, so why does he love me so much? I do not deserve his love.

As all these questions lingered in my mind, only one word was sufficient to answer these questions and clear up my confusion: Grace. It has always been his grace.

Plastic Surgery

As I was unable to take a real shower, techs had been giving me bed baths. One day a tech washed my left calf and asked if I'd hurt it before. He saw a long narrow black spot and wondered if it hurt when he pushed on it. It didn't; I just felt the pressure. I asked what was wrong with it. He said it was difficult to see until he washed the area, which explained why I hadn't noticed it. He reported it to a specialist to make sure it was not something serious.

Later that evening, a specialist came in and did a thorough examination. A doctor visited me the next day and told me that the black spot was a form of pressure sore which must be treated right away to make sure that it did not penetrate the bone. The pressure sore formed where that area always touched the metal guiding bar of my wheelchair which was adjacent to my left calf. He added that plastic surgery was needed to remove the pressure sore and to reconstruct the area immediately. In a few days, I was on the operating table once again. Thankfully, the surgery went well. The pressure sore had not penetrated the bone, which could have been fatal if it hadn't been removed right away. If the tech hadn't found the black spot that day, I would not have known about the pressure sore until I was sick again with a potentially severe form of infection and faced possible amputation or serious treatment that could be worse than the bed care.

Was this the reason that God allowed the tear on my esophagus and did not heal it immediately? Was it so the sore could be discovered and treated while I was already doing bed care? Or was I just trying to put the broken pieces of my life together and reinterpret them to sound amazing and inspiring when I shared my story with others? One way or another, this incident was also the result of God's grace, and I could not fathom the perfect timing of finding the pressure sore and being in the perfect place to diagnose and treat it. Even if I had found it at home and it had been removed, I would have gone through the cycle again. That would have been another awful experience to complain about and cause doubt in God.

By God's grace, I was able to endure the rest of the time in the hospital and was finally discharged. About two days before the discharge day, I took my first shower in almost three months. What I was hoping to hear from the surgeon each Monday never happened; however, I'd heard what I needed to hear from my heavenly Surgeon who operated and treated my spirit for almost three months. What did God want to accomplish through this time of fire? If it was to strengthen my spirit and faith, the mission was more than complete. But his mysterious mission was not over yet, unfortunately and thankfully.

Miracles

After I returned home from my nearly three-month hospitalization at Swedish Hospital, twenty or more medical bills welcomed my return. It felt like déjà vu of the 2005 nightmare. Back then I was still in the process of recovering from an infection and losing about twenty pounds, and was still on antibiotics and a feeding tube. But something was different this time. I had a small faith in God—probably smaller than a mustard seed—for I could not move any mountains. It was a faith deconstructed by challenges, doubt, and fear, but it was in the progress of being reconstructed through an infusion of God's grace. Using this small faith, God moved me to seek him and ask for his help with gratitude and humility.

God inspired me during my time of prayer and reflection to write letters to the people and organizations that had helped me in the hospital. At first I was skeptical that it would reduce the bills. But something was different this time. I thought surely God could move their hearts and inspire them to help me. Even if they did not change their minds, I had nothing to lose. And writing a letter also meant that I was fulfilling my duty as a person who appreciated their help. I started writing letters thanking them for their services, asking for their help with either canceling their medical bills or giving me a discount, and explaining to them about my financial situation and personal story of living with disability.

After two or three weeks passed by, dozens of letters were delivered to my house. My family was excited to open those letters. They stated that they were sorry to hear about my situation, that they appreciated my expression of gratitude, and had decided to cancel my medical bills. It was amazing. All of the bills except for two or three were canceled, even one bill that was about $600,000.

Dad's Surgery

About a week after I was discharged from Swedish Hospital, we became alarmed about Dad's health. We did not know what was going on but his laugh was worrisome and fake, one that was intended to calm our worries. Mom and I had observed since 2008 that he had had intestinal issues.

Dad's father had colon cancer in 2006; he underwent chemotherapy but passed away in 2007. We were concerned about what this family history could mean for Dad, but did not know what our next step should be. So we began with prayer.

It took some time, but we found the right person from CICP to guide us to the next step, which was for him to have a colonoscopy, a procedure we were unfamiliar with. We were all nervous, especially Dad, who wondered if he was repeating his Dad's experience with cancer. We prayed to God for mercy out of fear of cancer overcoming his health, body, even life, and destroying our family's life. We prayed for healing and for it not to be cancer. But if it was, we asked for him to provide a way to overcome it. We prayed for God to hold us together in faith, love, and strength.

The colonoscopy revealed a massive polyp in Dad's colon. When I asked the doctor if it was cancer, he responded that it was most likely cancer because of its size, but a biopsy had been ordered to examine it. He told me that someone would call me later to make an appointment for a CT scan to examine whether it had spread around his body. I could not believe what I just heard. Tears began wetting my face even before I had begun processing the meaning of the results, even though Mom and I had suspected the cause to be cancer. I knew that I had to tell Dad and once again it felt like déjà vu from when I had to tell him that I could never walk again.

With a heavy heart, I called him. His voice was very calm and gentle, as if he already knew what I was going to say. "They found a mass in your colon," I said, "and it is being tested right now. But it can be . . ." I trailed off. Dad probably noticed that my voice was trembling and finished the sentence for me: "It can be cancer." He went on, "Hey, don't worry. We can do this!" But as he was trying to cheer me up, I could also hear his tears and sorrow. "Yes, we can do this. Let's do this together with God," I said.

When I told Mom, she seemed somewhat bold, as if she already knew. She encouraged Dad and me to trust in God. Four days later, which felt like months, he received the CT scan results. The days had served as a time to prepare our hearts and faith in God. Perhaps this was the "appropriate" preparation needed for the worst scenario of metastatic cancer, which had claimed the life of my grandfather. They had, indeed, found cancer. But there was good news: it was not metastatic. The cancer was benign, not aggressive, and could be removed through surgery. We were told that it could have been growing for ten years, but because the cancer was benign, it had not spread beyond the colon.

After explaining this to my parents, we thanked God with tears of joy and praised his name. A few days later, a medical coordinator from CICP called me to talk about Dad's case. She told us that the next step was to schedule a meeting with a surgeon to have an operation and assured us that there was just enough funding to cover all the medical expenses. We could not believe it. We never expected them to offer any funding to support Dad. We could not stop thanking her and praising God for his mercy.

I told Lucy about this incident and the possibility of not having a caregiver until his recovery, which could take weeks. Craig Hospital decided to help me by paying for three caregivers a day for two weeks. Five years had passed since a caregiver besides Dad had helped me, so I was somewhat worried about the sudden change. Thankfully, they came to my house on time and helped me as we asked them. The first came in the morning and helped me with eating breakfast, dropping me off at the light rail station, and picking me up to bring me back home. The second caregiver came in the afternoon, helped me with taking showers and transferring me to bed. The third caregiver helped me with using the toilet at night and eating because I was doing bed care by then, following the routine of transferring to my bed after staying in my wheelchair for eight hours. I was relieved and felt confident that I could wait until Dad fully recovered while also realizing and appreciating how he had become the perfect caregiver for me because he was fully trained to help me. He knew my exact needs, limitations, and wants, and loved me with all his heart and strength.

Dad's surgery went well and the results of the biopsy meant that Dad did not need chemotherapy. There was another round of praising God. He had been meeting all our needs according to Paul's testimony in Phil 4:19: "And my God will meet all your needs according to the riches of his glory in Christ Jesus." Otherwise, how could CICP have provided the exact financial resources that my family needed at the time of our request? The timing could not have been more perfect. Also, Lucy was able to find extra funding to hire techs at the right time, otherwise we could not have managed to find and pay for them. How about the discounts on and cancelations of the medical bills? How about the perfect timing of finding the pressure sore and being at the perfect place to treat and heal it? Yes, God used many people and organizations to meet my needs, but to doubt his intentional intervention and to consider it luck was insulting to him at that stage of my journey with him. I experienced too many incidents and too much of his love to question his provision of my needs and his grace upon my family. As

Brandon Heath's song says, there was no turning back from Jesus starting from that moment.

Clean Credit Score

There were many times that I had thought about filing for bankruptcy because I did not want to add additional financial burden on my parents. About a year after my accident, I brought my concerns to my parents. They thanked me for my concern, but as many medical organizations had done so much to help me after my accident, they suggested that even though they couldn't repay the bills right away, we could do our best to pay them until we could not. Despite our difficult financial situation, we split up the monthly payments and paid ten or twenty dollars a month. The amount of money that I owed could not be paid off in seven years by paying the minimum monthly payment, though I was able to pay off my debt for a few of them. After making minimum payments for five or more years, a few of the collection agencies seemed to cancel my debts. Maybe they recognized that I was trying my best to repay my debt.

When I had an opportunity to open a credit card account, I was somewhat doubtful that I could get one because of my debt to collection agencies. Without much expectation, when I registered with Experian to check my credit score, I saw that my credit score was 750! I could not believe what I saw and thought that the website must be fraudulent. I regretted registering my personal information there. But I tried other top credit bureaus which also showed similar credit scores. Skeptically, after making a few more calls to my bank and those credit bureaus, I was finally convinced that it was my real credit score.

Part 6

New Dream

God had given me a new dream for my life. Instead of pursuing a worldly lifestyle, I wanted to pursue Jesus. I wanted to minister to others, to share my story and tell others what Jesus had done for me. I wanted others to know of my newfound hope. During the years that I dreamed of becoming a sushi chef and attaining a wealthy lifestyle, I never would have imagined I would find myself back in school—certainly not by choice, and certainly not to learn more about God! Getting an education had seemed like a waste of time and money before, but things were different now. God changed my heart and now I found myself dreaming his dreams for me.

Gratitude

My life was overflowing with gratitude. Experiencing God's provision was amazing. My prayers started with thanksgiving and finished with thanksgiving. I did not need to say anything else; expressing my gratitude was more than enough. I became confident in my faith in God and his love for me. The more I read the Bible and reflected on its teaching on my salvation, the deeper my gratitude became for the suffering and death of Jesus on the cross. Every time I reflected on the cross of Jesus I was truly amazed. I was blown away by the truth that the eternal, glorious, and powerful God chose to create the world and human beings, have personal relationships with them, invite them to have eternal fellowship with him, and become a man in order to accomplish his awesome and great plans for humanity.

Although it took some time to understand difficult texts in the Bible, I believed that my salvation was anchored in Jesus, the Son of God.

As I was reading the Gospels, the verse about Jesus asking Peter the following question captured my attention: "Do you love me?" Jesus asked him this question three times, and three times Peter answered without any hesitation that he did. But surprisingly, when I asked the question of myself, I couldn't say it with full confidence. I was thankful for his love and help over the years, but saying "I love you" was difficult. It wasn't that I did not love him, it just did not feel authentic and strong enough. I felt like I was saying it reluctantly without a sincere and truthful heart, as if I was giving God lip service. It was a horrible feeling. God was telling me that he loved me so much that he gave his life for me, but all I could do was say "Thank You."

I knew that to love God was the most appropriate, ethical, and moral response to a Being who gave his life for me and to whom I confessed was my God, King, and Master. I knew that obedience was one of the greatest commandments and the response that he expected from me dearly. I knew intellectually that I should love him, but my love felt only halfhearted. I felt so guilty that I felt like a traitor. I prayed to God through tears and told him how sorry I was for not having such a heart. At that moment I prayed, "Help me to love you with all my heart, strength, and spirit. Help me to love you the most, more than anybody."

Although it took some time, God graciously answered my prayer and I was able to say "I love you, God" with confidence, joy, and gratitude. My love for him became deeper and more enriched because of his amazing love for me. There was a time when I shared my faith journey with one of my fellow graduate students, and she called me a "Jesus freak" in a very nice and respectful way, and I loved it. I wanted to be a Jesus freak and to love him all the days of my life, whether I had what I asked of him or not and whether I had to go through fire, water, or on paved ways. To love God became my dream.

Since the day God gave me Jeremiah 33:3, which was written on a poster and pinned on the wall of my study room, it lingered in my thoughts and I recited it hundreds of times: "Call unto me, and I will answer thee, and shew thee great and mighty things, which thou knowest not" (KJV). I had to ask, "What is God's plans for me? What does God want to show me?" My future truly seemed dark and gloomy. I couldn't see anything ahead of me. Having no job, money, legal status, or college degree, I was afraid to know what my future held. I wasn't sure if I was ready to dream something new and I wasn't sure whether I was ready to stop daydreaming about my broken one. "What if I fail again? What if my new dream falls apart?" Over the years I had learned that while my self-centered and ambitious dreams could fail, God's dream would never fail and would always prevail in all circumstances. I prayed that I may dream what he dreams and chase after them, although I may not understand, agree with, or like its course and design.

I did not yet hear or see any new dreams, but I kept reciting his words and promises. I didn't know the purpose of living with a disability, why I had the snowboarding accident that day, or why God was not healing my injury. I didn't know about God's specific future plans for me but knew what I had to do each day: spend time with God in prayer, read and reflect on his words, praise his name, and obey his commands. This was to focus on the best gift that I already received from God, not on the things that I did not have. It was to love God with all my heart, strength, and spirit. I was not sure if I could do them for many years, but I could try to do my best each day.

One day, during my devotions, I sensed strong confirmation that God was glorified by my daily commitments and obedience and he taught me that they were indeed his plans for me. At first it seemed too simple and basic to be viewed as God's plan. I thought they had to be big and fancy. What I considered small, he considered great, and what I considered great, he considered small. Surely those basics were the foundation upon which God wanted to establish and build more of his plans, just as Jesus taught his disciples that those who hear his teachings and obey them are like those who built their houses on the rock (Matt 7:25–26). Jesus suffered and died on the cross to bring me closer to him and to have a personal relationship with him every day. And I was in this gracious fellowship with him. Such confirmation was what I needed to continue my journey with him without having to know his specific future plans. If a sinner like me could somehow please my Lord and King, I was ready to do it repeatedly.

Calling to Help Others

In the process of seeking God's plans, he gave me the desire to help people who experience suffering and have been impacted by disability. At first I was not certain whether this desire was from God or not. I wondered, "I am the one who needs help from others and still struggle with many problems and unresolved issues. How can a person like me help those in need? What can I offer them? How can I give hope and encouragement to those who have been broken by unanswered prayers and want healing? Would they take me seriously? What message can I give them?" As I began to pay attention to the stories of others, I observed that bitterness, anger, frustration, disappointment, isolation, blame, and suffering were everywhere and actually the common experience of humanity, although people experienced suffering differently in their different contexts.

Deep inside I felt that I could help others at least in a small way. Indeed, I was a professional sufferer and knew a thing or two about the impact of suffering on individuals' lives and their relationships with God, though that is not to say that I understood or had experienced all types of pain and suffering. Such desire to help others was inspired within my selfishness; therefore, I knew that God sowed the desire within my heart. It was gradually nurtured by the love and compassion that I received from many organizations and people who helped me over the years, which motivated me to give back.

The small, uncertain, and immature desire grew and finally became my new dream, which led to discovering God's calling to serve him and his people as a minister. I was still hesitant to accept the call. I wondered what I would say to people when they asked why I was still paralyzed if God is almighty and hears our prayers. I wondered if Christians would accept me as a minister or if they would prefer someone healthier who would be capable of physically helping and serving the congregation? Would I even be healthy enough to teach and preach the word of God? With so many old church buildings that are not wheelchair accessible, how could I serve God and his people as a minister? As I prayed for discernment over these questions, and even denied the calling from God for weeks and months, God confirmed it. I was worried about my weakness and limitation and the things that I could not do, while he was waiting for me to trust in his strength and limitless compassion and goodness and the things that he could do through my weakness and ministry. At last, I humbly, graciously, and fearfully accepted it and chose the Evangelical Presbyterian Church (EPC) through which to become a minister and to reaffirm my calling through the process of ordination, initiated and supervised by the EPC.

Furthering My Education

God began inspiring me with the desire to pursue further education after five years of working on my undergraduate degree. In 2011 I graduated from the University of Colorado Denver with a major in psychology and minor in sociology and started a master's program in pastoral and spiritual care at Iliff School of Theology at Denver. The institution underscored liberal theological ideas compared to my conservative, Korean Christian background; however, I was able to learn the importance of thinking widely and of respecting different traditions and theological and secular understandings. While attending the school, I met Rev. Jae Son. We were in the same degree program and ended up participating in the same hospital chaplaincy clinical pastoral education (CPE) program for five months or so. We met on a weekly basis with our CPE supervisor and its members, worked as volunteer chaplains at Porter Adventist Hospital, and completed the chaplain program together. We became friends and ministry partners, and his family and my family built a close relationship over the years.

Hyperreflexia

I had another bout with hyperreflexia in 2012. I felt chills in my body. At first I just thought I was under the weather. Chills turned into shivering, which soon turned into discomfort. The discomfort became pain in my upper body where I have the most sensation. More than that, I had a severe headache, as if someone was pounding my forehead with a hammer. The pain was more severe than the time I was stuck in the MRI tube. I felt so sick and was in so much pain as if my head was about to blow off. I knew that I was having hyperreflexia and knew that it was urgent, so I called the Craig Hospital hotline. The nurse suggested that my catheter was blocked by urine sediments or bladder stones. If so, it needed to be changed as soon as possible.

Dad was able to change the suprapubic catheter right away, and when he pulled out the catheter and inserted a new one, just as the nurse had suggested, urine that had been blocked by sediments rushed out. Soon my pounding headache, body pain, high blood pressure, and body temperature subsided, but a minor headache and neck and shoulder pain remained for a few days. The nurse from Craig called to check on me and explained that the blockage of the catheter could be related to bladder stones, sediments, and infection, and that it was normal for people with spinal cord injuries and suprapubic catheters to have them.

She asked when I'd had my last cystoscopy. I didn't know what that was, and after she explained that it was a procedure to look inside the urinary bladder, I knew I had never had one before. Neither had I had an annual evaluation at Craig Hospital where I should have been receiving yearly examinations, consultations with occupational therapists to discuss new occupational equipment, and physical therapists to discuss different exercise and rehabilitation options.

I called Lucy to explain my issue and she was able to arrange an appointment for the cystoscopy. About a week later, I was back at Craig Hospital in one of its outpatient exam rooms. A urologist explained that he would examine my bladder and remove any bladder stones, and warned me that I would need to endure the discomfort and pain for about an hour. As much as I hated the pain of changing suprapubic catheters, I hated the procedure even more. Unlike some parts of my body that have dull sensations, my suprapubic area has hyper sensation; I feel pain there every day. But I was grateful to receive the procedure and have bladder stones removed so that I would not suffer with and die of hyperreflexia. I decided to suck it up and to face it with gratitude and joy. Extracting the bladder stones was extremely painful. There were about fifteen black bladder stones, and I asked him to save them as a souvenir.

Life Is Unfair

I was relieved and grateful to have received the procedure, but at the same time I was bitter about having to go through the unpleasant experience because of my spinal cord injury. "Life with disability surely requires high maintenance," I thought. "Is it fair that people like me have to live with this kind of extra burden? I could have died if the catheter had not been replaced right away. Is life supposed to be like this? Am I still naïve to think that life must be fair for all people?" But then I reflected on the fact that God is fair. He did not create this world to be unfair. And what great things had I done to deserve God's fairness? My good deeds could never be enough to demand his fairness. Perhaps I was expecting too much from this world. Perfection does not exist in this corrupt world. My eyes and hope should be set on God's eternal kingdom that he would establish on earth just as it is in heaven. Yes, good things may happen in this world, but perfection exists only in the kingdom of God. Thankfully, God, who is always fair, knew the unfairness that I was experiencing daily and was with me, helping me put my hope in his eternal kingdom.

New Wheelchair

A year after I started my studies at Iliff School of Theology, Lucy emailed me about a potential opportunity to receive a new electric wheelchair. In 2012 I was still using the used electric wheelchair donated by Craig Hospital in 2005. It was a great machine but it had a few mechanical issues. So I agreed to have my name put on the list. My family was super excited as we could not afford one without insurance. Electric wheelchairs are considered necessary medical equipment for people with paralysis, so it can be supported financially by insurance companies. We turned to God, the CEO of our insurance company. A few weeks later we were shocked that I was selected as the 2012 recipient of a new electric wheelchair provided by the Darrell Gwynn Foundation. Gwynn was a world champion drag racer during the 1980s who had a racing accident in 1990 and became a paraplegic. After the incident, he founded the Darrell Gwynn Foundation and teamed with Craig Hospital to donate new wheelchairs to low-income people with spinal cord injuries.

At Craig Hospital I saw a physical therapist who took my measurements and I also got to try out different types of wheelchairs. There were front wheelers, mid-wheelers, and rear wheelers. Rear wheelers were the most powerful and durable for outdoor driving with the least mechanical issues, whereas the mid-wheelers and front wheelers had more finesse in making sharp turns and corners in tight and small office settings. By that point I was a student and had no issues making sharp turns at home, so I chose the rear wheeler with the most horsepower and the fewest mechanical issues. It looked great and had at least 1.5 horsepower and the options to tilt the whole seat of the wheelchair and to recline only the back seat of the chair, like reclining a car seat.

After about seven weeks passed by, there was my new wheelchair wrapped in a plastic bag with a price tag of $14,000. I received deep inspiration from Gwynn. I found out later that Gwynn had been supporting people with paralysis even before his traumatic race accident and courageously continued his philanthropy after the incident.

Cherry Hills Community Church

After worshiping at home with my family for several years, I started attending Cherry Hills Community Church in 2013. I served its special needs ministry, received callings to serve people with disabilities, and met sincere friends and believers. They chose to see me as a person and brother in Christ, not as wheelchair, disability, bad luck, or limitation. There was a time when they invited me to hike at Staunton State Park and arranged a track-chair, a specialized wheelchair designed to function outdoors. Although it was an uncomfortable riding experience, I had an exciting time hanging out with them and enjoying the beautiful nature of the forest, my first outdoor experience after the accident.

Denver Seminary

In 2013, after graduating from Illif School of Theology, I started the ordination process with the EPC. I decided to apply to Denver Seminary to receive a Master of Divinity degree from an evangelical institution. Certain institutions did not accept undocumented students, so I had to make sure that Denver Seminary would accept me. I met with Dr. Sung Wook Chung, a Christian theology professor, to talk about the possibility of attending Denver Seminary. He told me that it welcomes all students regardless of their immigration status. My journey at Denver Seminary began without conflict, and Dr. Chung became my mentor, ministry partner, and friend.

In the process of seeking God's will during my graduate studies, many questions concerning human suffering and disabilities and their relationship with God lingered in my thoughts. I had many questions such as what was the meaning of human suffering? Where does suffering come from? Is human suffering the direct result of personal sins or the effect of the sin of Adam and Eve? What does human suffering mean for God? How does he respond to it? Can God, who is all-powerful and all-knowing, experience any sort of affliction and vulnerability like human beings who are finite and limited in their strength and knowledge? If he has a personal relationship with his people and loves them dearly, but their suffering does not move him without causing himself any pain, what kind of relationship do human creatures have with their very Creator who made them in his image and likeness? On the other hand, if God suffers like his creatures who often suffer because of their vulnerability and ontological limitation, can he really save them from their suffering and be called a God at all?

Further, why did my snowboarding accident happen? Did God foreknow of the horrific event and have the authority to prevent it from happening? If he did, why did he not prevent me from going to the mountain that day? Did God try to stop me through my parents and friends the night before the accident? Why should my parents suffer so much pain because of the choice I made? Is there any meaning in my suffering or their suffering? What is the meaning of the suffering of believers and that of his church and churches? How should his churches respond to the suffering of the world? If he is good and almighty, why does evil exist in this world? Why does God allow suffering and evil in this world? Does God have plans for his created world? Is expecting and submitting to his plans worth the patience, prayer, and suffering of believers?'

Ordination

Many events happened in 2016 as if it was the year of harvest. One was my ordination. The process of ordination by the EPC had begun in 2014, and Rev. Sharon Beekmann was my guide and mentor who walked with me throughout the rigorous process and encouraged me to serve my calling. We met monthly and talked about our journeys with Jesus, ordination preparation, and ministry visions. Her experiences with suffering and spiritual battle helped me to reframe my suffering as a positive means to connect to people and to use it to build my ministry. After preaching at Hope Church in 2016 and receiving the acceptance letter from the university, I felt confirmation that God was leading me along the right path to serve him as my family had been praying for a long time. In May 2016, I graduated from Denver Seminary with a Master of Divinity with a concentration in theology. After years of preparation for and passing the verbal and written ordination exams, I was ordained by the EPC in September.

J. D. Kim Ministries

Another significant event in 2016 was launching J. D. Kim Ministries during my final semester at Denver Seminary after God confirmed my calling in the spring of 2016. J. D. Kim Ministries is a nonprofit Christian organization which was God's dream. He dreams of the day when people of all colors, abilities, ages, social statuses, disabilities, genders, cultures, and levels of wealth and suffering will join his everlasting and fortified Kingdom to praise Jesus as their Lord and Savior; worship the Father, Son, and Holy Spirit; and have eternal fellowship of love, holiness, and joy with him. There will be no tears or suffering, only the sound of his angels and saints singing, "Holy, holy, holy is the Lord God Almighty!"

J. D. Kim Ministries therefore seeks to share the good news of the Lord Jesus with all people. It envisions the true body of Jesus Christ reaching out to individuals experiencing the hopelessness and helplessness of living without hope in the true Liberator, bearing suffering with fellow believers as different parts of the body of Jesus Christ, and glorifying the Creator of the universe, the triune God. Dr. Rich Sweeney, Dr. Sung Wook Chung, Rev. Jae Son, Dr. Dick Elliot, and Dad are the board members.

J. D. Kim Ministries has three ministry areas. The first is teaching Christian theology. So many believers and non-believers undergo theological crises which often negatively impact their relationship with God. Therefore, the ministry seeks to teach healthy and balanced Christian theology rooted in the truth of Scripture and of evangelical theology. The second ministry area is encouragement. I share my personal testimony and the ups and downs, including my vulnerability, limitations, and sorrow. If we can share our suffering with others, we can bear our pain together in Christ. If we can share the joy, gratitude, and struggle of our pilgrimages, we can bear our crosses and partake in the journey together. I preach the message of the gospel, for it is the only hope of humanity trapped in the endless cycle of sin and suffering. The third ministry area supports people impacted by disabilities. Many have been mistreated and neglected by believers and non-believers for a long time. My ministry attempts to encourage people impacted by disabilities, provide resources to disability ministries, and to communicate God's mission and dream for reaching out to and serve people who are marginalized in this world.

Preaching at Hope Church

Yet another significant of 2016 was being asked to speak at Hope Church in Cordova, Tennessee. Pastor Rufus Smith, who was a teaching elder of the EPC and the senior pastor of Hope Church, heard me share my testimony at one of the Presbytery meetings of the EPC. Afterward he approached me about traveling to Memphis to share my testimony at his church, adding that he felt that the Holy Spirit had moved him to ask. So I simply said, "Yes, I will be there." It would be the first time my family had driven out of Colorado since my accident, and was actually the first time we had taken a vacation in twelve years. The trip from Denver would take about twenty hours because my modified van could not go over sixty-five miles per hour. Driving to the east coast was somewhat complicated by our not having phones with navigation systems. We thought of it as a mission trip. After all, we reasoned, the apostle Paul walked about 1,600 miles during his first mission trip and it took him fifty-three days. We were sure we could make the 1,100-mile journey by car. My van was packed with my medical supplies and we were filled with excitement and joy.

We arrived after two days of driving and the church staff—and Pastor Smith's assistant, Fee, in particular—welcomed my family and served us like a royal family. I preached in front of thousands of people on Saturday evening and three times on Sunday morning. I had shared my testimony in front of a few hundred people before, but never thousands. God strengthened me to boldly preach the message of God's love. After the worship services, many people approached me to share their gratitude and kind and encouraging words. On the way back to Denver, although tired physically, we overflowed with the Spirit and thanksgiving.

Doctoral Program Acceptance

Once home, a letter accepting me into the PhD program at the University of Aberdeen in the UK awaited me. When I told my parents about the letter, tears of gratitude and joy showered our faces and we held each other and praised the Lord. I began the program with doctoral supervisor Dr. Paul Nimmo. Even though distance students were normally required to visit the campus a few times a year and meet with their supervisors in person, after hearing about my physical condition and its implications on traveling and finding housing there, my supervisor and the director of the post-graduate program allowed me to complete my doctoral program long distance. It was the best accommodation that I could have received from the academic institution.

When I had talked to Dr. Chung about my questions during my independent study under his supervision at Denver Seminary, he told me that answering these questions was a lifelong project, not a project for one semester. He persistently encouraged me to pursue a doctoral degree in theology, but at that point I was not interested and figured it wouldn't be possible anyway because most of the doctoral programs in the US required residency. It would mean a move for my whole family if I were to pursue doctoral work. But he had suggested exploring doctoral programs in Europe because some did not require residency under certain circumstances. Gradually his encouragement influenced my passive attitude, and after long and sincere prayer in search of my passion and interest, I reconsidered doctoral research.

I sensed that God was moving me to pursue a doctorate to answer my questions about suffering—not only for my own curiosity and benefit, but also for others who struggle to answer these questions and go through various daily hardships. I finally accepted that pursuing a doctoral degree was God's plan for me and decided that my new lifelong project must begin with exploring questions related to God and human suffering.

In this way, my doctoral research began on the doctrine of divine impassibility, a particular Christian doctrine that deals with God's response to and relationship with human suffering. My research attempted to answer whether God was capable of being associated with suffering and of being moved by the world and to explore whether—and if so, how—the triune God, who is both almighty and all-loving, responds to his beloved human creatures who were made in his image and yet who are now implicated in sin and suffering. I sensed that pursuing this path was God's dream for me and prayed that I may be used for his glory.

Immigration Status

Understanding the necessity of having legal status to live in this country, I reached out to an immigration lawyer to discuss the possibility of pursuing legal status again. He suggested reaching out to United States Citizenship and Immigration Services (USCIS) to request deferred action which provides temporary immigration status to undocumented immigrants for certain cases. It enables recipients to work and reside in the US legally and to receive driver's licenses and state identification. However, it does not offer any medical or government support or pathways to permanent residency or citizenship and requires that I reapply for the program every two years once I receive it. If I traveled outside the country, I would not be able to return.

My application for deferred action was approved. Many thanks to the lawyer and his team and to fifty of my friends who wrote kind letters to the immigration office, affirming that I was a good person who can be of benefit to many people living in this country. But we ran into a challenge when it was time to renew my status. The president had signed an executive order to slow down the immigration process. A process that usually took three months for approval when there were no issues was not moving forward even after twelve months. My lawyer said that we could only wait for the review process to be completed and that there was nothing else we could do to facilitate the process.

After waiting for almost two years, my non-Christian lawyer called me to inform me that my renewal application was approved and said the following: "Mr. Kim, I have seen many applications rejected and delayed longer than your application because of the presidential executive order, so I thought your application would be rejected as well. But somehow yours was approved. Seeing and hearing about the things that have been happening in your life, some sort of god is watching out for you." I praised the mighty name of Jesus. In this way, I was approved to live in this country with a valid immigration status for the first time since I became an undocumented immigrant in 2004. Consequently, although not as a legal resident or American citizen, I was able to work and live in this country without anxiety and fear of deportation.

I am one of the millions of dreamers waiting and praying for a legal pathway to US citizenship. I have been living in this country for almost twenty-five years; all my friends and most of my family members reside here. I speak English and know the history, politics, culture, and sports of this country. I serve churches, non-profit organizations, believers and non-believers, and people of all colors, with and without disabilities, living in the US. I have been paying my state and federal taxes diligently. Despite these things, I am still not an American citizen. Along with many of my fellow dreamers, I simply want to live among our friends, family, and co-workers, and work legally in this country. I have much respect and admiration for this nation and her people and constitution; I desire nothing more than the best for this nation.

Doctoral Program Challenges

The journey of the doctoral program was met with many unexpected difficulties. After starting my doctoral program in 2016, I experienced several physical hardships such as blood clots, bladder stones, hyperreflexia, a broken wheelchair, just to name a few. In 2017, my wheelchair was broken and needed to be repaired immediately, but I had to wait for almost three months because of mistakes on the part of the repair company. During that time I was using a loaned wheelchair that did not fit my body. That meant I was in a very uncomfortable and awkward position all day for three months. It was an awful experience. When I was crying out to God about being uncomfortable and in pain, he moved my heart to think about those in certain countries who do not even have such chairs and who literally live on the streets. Joni Eareckson Tada has written about visiting those places and seeing their suffering. The description of her observation became vivid images in my mind, and God used the images to teach me that helping those with disabilities without wheelchairs around the world was his dream for me and my ministry.

Unfortunately, being in an awkward position in the wheelchair impacted my blood circulation and led to a second episode of DVT. One day I found my right thigh swollen and headed to the hospital for an ultrasound. Within a few hours, I was hospitalized for surgery to get the blood clots out of my thigh and abdomen areas. The surgeon told me that the blood clots traveled close to my lungs, so I had been wise to come to the ER quickly. After the surgery, the doctor told me that I must take blood thinning medication for the rest of my life.

After my first major episode of hyperreflexia in 2011, I might've had one or two. But in 2018 alone I had at least six episodes. I had tried everything I could do to prevent bladder stones from causing further problems. But my best effort was not enough to stop the growth of the bacteria and sediment in my poor bladder. The bladder infection caused by the bladder stones and bacteria manifested in a fever, which lasted at least a week or so. The side effects of hyperreflexia were the most difficult to endure, especially the indescribable pain of a pounding headache and body aches. There were a few times when I thought I would meet Jesus in paradise soon.

In 2018 I had to have a bladder stone removal procedure without surgery and anesthesia. As before, the procedure was painful but bearable. As I began having hyperreflexia, my blood pressure skyrocketed to 230, my temperature went over 100, I developed a rash all over my body, and the procedure had to be stopped. The doctor was not able to remove all the stones, and he'd had to break some of them up to remove them. He recommended surgery, which was too expensive for me. Thankfully, Rich Sweeney started fundraising through GoFundMe, and many of my friends made financial contributions to raise the exact amount of funding needed to pay for the surgery. In March 2020, just before the COVID-19 outbreak, I had another bladder stone removal surgery under anesthesia.

And the doctoral program itself was more difficult than I anticipated. Every two weeks for more than a year, I submitted a progress report, reading plan, and research reflection to my doctoral supervisor, Dr. Paul Nimmo, and had a meeting with him via Skype. He was always humble and gracious in his supervision and helped me to think clearly and deeply. When I experienced writer's block, I reached out to Dr. Sung Wook Chung and his wife, Dr. In Kyung Chung, who advised me to focus on the whole project because I often got lost in the details. Hearing about their experiences and receiving their advice helped me to proceed with my research project. When COVID-19 hit the whole world in early 2020, I was finishing up my dissertation, and by God's grace and with the help of my friends and mentors who consistently prayed for me and encouraged me, I was able to submit my dissertation, pass the viva voce (doctoral oral examination), and cross the finish line in 2021. If God had told me in 2006 that his educational plan for me would take fourteen years, I would not have taken the opportunity. Perhaps certain things should be hidden until the right time.

Since 2016 I have served Craig Hospital as a volunteer chaplain and occasionally lead worship services. I have been teaching Christian theology courses in both English and Korean at Denver Seminary since 2020 and started a new position as Assistant Director of Doctor of Ministry Korean Studies Program at the seminary. My first book on the suffering of God, entitled *Constructing a Mediating Theology: Affirming the Impassibility and the Passibility of the Triune God,* was published in 2022 and is based on my doctoral dissertation. In this book, I argue that God does not experience any suffering in himself, but rather chooses to suffer in his relationship with his beloved creatures. It is my sincere hope that I could write another book on the theology of suffering that explains the way in which the suffering of God is connected to the discipleship and fellowship of believers and the mission and ministry of the church of God.

Concluding Thought

Never in a million years would I have thought that I would be reading the Bible, teaching theology courses, and writing a testimonial book in which I boast about my vulnerability and my Lord Jesus. This is not my dream; it is God's dream. Even after eighteen years, there are moments when I wonder whether I am still dreaming or not. For ten years I used to slap my face, wanting to wake up from the nightmare. But now I know that I am dreaming God's dream and often slap my face to push harder to follow his dream.

Since the snowboarding accident, I am still paralyzed and have no new movement; however, God's dream moves me despite my paralysis. My hands are reaching towards people who are going through hardship. My mouth preaches the message of the gospel of Jesus Christ and praises his mighty and loving name. My body is with those bodies impaired and paralyzed and with God's people working together to glorify his name. Along with many Christians around the world, my feet are marching on the boulevard of my broken dream to declare that it has been restored to God's dream by the blood of Jesus, and also declare that his dream can regenerate our broken identity, hope, and dream and can make us laugh again, live again, and dream again.

I am chasing the Dreamer who always accomplishes his dreams and wheeling with he who will glorify my broken body one day and bring me to the eternal house that he prepared for me. There I will be free to move my arms and legs and walk again. There I will forever serve my parents with the love that they demonstrated through their sacrifices on earth and hang out with my friends, my brothers and sisters in Christ. There I will praise my Lord and Savior all the days along with numerous saints who endured hardships of suffering and chronic conditions and disabilities. Just as Jesus had scars on his side, hands, and feet, we will bear the marks of our suffering—which will not be the marks of shame, curse, or vulnerability, but rather glorious marks demonstrating our faith, endurance, and victory in Jesus's name. We will be sharing the stories of our weaknesses and boasting of the strength and grace of our God, which was more than enough in times of physical, psychological, and spiritual troubles.

All of the people and caregivers who showed compassion to the marginalized will be served by the recipients of their compassion and caregiving and celebrated with all the saints and angels in our Master's eternal fellowship in heaven and on the newly reconstructed earth. There, no further "remodeling" or "accessibility" will be needed. There, I will spend my eternity with my Caregiver who has placed me on the chariot of fire, protecting me with his hundreds of angels who have been pushing my wheelchair from behind, pulling it from the front, walking beside me, residing within me, and watching over me from above. To the Father, Son, and Holy Spirit, I give you every part of my life and each of my breaths. Let me live and die for you every day until the day you take me home or come again to judge the world once and for all. All I want to hear from you is "Great job! My good and faithful servant!"

Epilogue

Eighteen years have passed since the day my life changed dramatically. I thought that I would walk out of Craig Hospital within three months, but I didn't. I thought I would try out the Christian faith for one year, and if there was no healing, I would opt out. Just before the expiration date, I decided to try my best for another two years, thinking that even the disciples of Jesus were with him for three years until they became super saints and received the power and authority to heal the sick and to cast out demons in Jesus's name. Three years passed. No supernatural healing happened, but I found myself following Jesus in my wheelchair. My body was still paralyzed and stuck on a wheelchair, but my spirit was as free as it could be, sitting on the invisible chariot of fire prepared by God. I was immature in many aspects after the accident, and if God had told me then that I would not be able to move my body even after eighteen long years, I would not have begun my journey with Jesus and would have given up my faith a long time ago. Somehow, my daily walk with Jesus led me to seek what he wants from me to this day. In my journey with him he has been with me always, holding me with his righteous right hand as he promised, even though I tried to let go of him. That is the only reason I am still wheeling with him.

Before I conclude this book, I want to share with you how I interpret my snowboarding accident and the stories that happened afterward, and answer many questions that lingered in my thoughts for a long time. You may agree or disagree with my answers and interpretation. They may help you to answer the questions that bothered and depressed you for a long time. They may encourage you to live with whatever conditions robbed you of confidence and to put your hope in Jesus Christ and start your journey with him. Or they may actually discourage you, and if this is this case I apologize sincerely, for the intent of this book was always to share my faith journey as honestly as possible in order to demonstrate that walking with

Jesus is not a silver bullet for resolving problems and receiving healing and seeing miracles. However, I know they have helped me and are still helping me to survive hardships in this world.

My self-centered dreams were deconstructed by God. I am using the term "deconstruction" in the context of physical construction of a building, as a planned and careful process of disassembling the parts of the building for reconstruction. God foreknew that I would exercise freedom to drive to Aspen the night before the accident and to choose to go snowboarding on that day and at that time and that the choices would lead to unfortunate and painful consequences. The result of the exercise of my sinful freedom was destruction, at least for me, without meaning and purpose. However, fully knowing the consequences of my free choices, God chose to allow the accident to happen that day—having good and special purposes and plans in mind for me—and used what appeared to be pure tragedy, evil, and destruction as a means of his deconstruction of my life. He was so confident that he would accomplish his plans which would glorify his holy name and benefit me in a number of ways that he chose to allow disability to be part of my life and to permit suffering to torment me momentarily in this world. He foreknew the extent of the suffering that I would experience and prepared the means to provide for my needs and to walk with me in the water and fire, understanding every inch of my distress and bearing it with me.

In the process of his deconstruction, God did not stop me from making such choices because he gave human beings the right to exercise freedom. Simultaneously, he is able to exercise his sovereignty over human freedom because he is the Creator of his creatures. That is, even if I want to choose option "A," God is able and has the divine right to move me to choose option "B." This sovereign act over human freedom seems to violate the exercise of human freedom. However, it is important to note that God, who foreknows the infinite number of the free choices of human beings, exercises his sovereignty using and respecting human freedom. If God did not foreknow the snowboarding accident, the accident would be simply a tragedy without any meaning and purpose. If he had nothing to do with it and was powerless to know its consequences, such a God would not be all-powerful and all-knowing and would not be able to answer many hours of my prayers. He wouldn't be accused of being part of my tragedy, but I would not seek him to resolve my hardship and suffering and to answer my prayers. I would not praise and worship him as my God. If God can also have an accident, who is going to encourage and rescue him?

Epilogue

Let me explain this relationship between God's sovereignty and the exercise of human freedom by referencing the famous story of Joseph from the Bible. Joseph had dreams of his family bowing down to him and repeatedly chose to tell his brothers about them, which seemed arrogant to them. His choice was naïve, almost innocent. Joseph's father was aware of the complicated sibling rivalries among the brothers and their jealousy of Joseph, and yet chose to send Joseph to check up on them. His decision was unwise, even inconsiderate. His brothers chose to sell their brother to the merchants for eight ounces of silver, knowing the possible hardships that he could face. It was an immoral and evil choice. Potiphar's wife falsely accused Joseph of mistreating and harassing her, and Potiphar chose to imprison him as punishment; the Pharaoh's cupbearer remembered Joseph and chose to tell the Pharaoh about Joseph when he had a prophetic dream concerning a future famine in Egypt. Pharaoh, upon hearing Joseph's interpretation of the dream even before the harvest began in Egypt, chose him as second in importance after him and put him in charge over the whole affairs and land of Egypt. In the end, God saved many Egyptians and others around Egypt and the families of Isaac through Joseph.

Each of these individuals made their own choices without being forced into them by anything or anyone, and a few of them even made evil and wicked decisions to harm Joseph. However, without wasting any of their choices, God used them to work out and accomplish his glorious plans. Joseph's God was feared and worshipped by the people, and his family and all the people around Egypt were spared under his leadership because Joseph had been trained to be the leader of Egypt culturally, socially, spiritually, and politically. The training was for the very purpose of saving people. For these reasons, during the famine when Joseph once again met his brothers who had betrayed him, he told them, "You intended to harm me, but God intended it for good to accomplish what is now being done, the saving of many lives" (Gen 50:20). In this way, God is able to use the choices of human beings to accomplish his glorious, sovereign, and foreknown plans. Although human beings can make evil, naïve, and sinful choices, God wills good in them.

My dream and life were completely deconstructed. My body was broken; my family was broken; my identity was broken; my relationships with people and church were broken; my faith and hope were broken; every part of my life was broken. Darkness and dust filled the deconstructed sight. It seemed so completely devastated that picking up all the broken pieces of my dream seemed useless. I was not able to let go of my past or my original dream; I tried to pick up those broken pieces and bled physically and internally. The more I struggled to rebuild the dream, the more I experienced failure, disappointment, and hopelessness. After the snowboard accident, when I reached out to God and asked if he could do anything about my miserable life, he held my hands and placed deep inside of me the stone that builders rejected which became the cornerstone of his new dream (Ps 118:22; Matt 21:42). As I began putting my faith and hope in God, he commanded me to call out to him for his great and mighty dreams. In the midst of my shaky journey with God that was filled with disappointment, uncertainty, and doubt, he continuously upheld me with his righteous right hand to keep me from falling and confirmed for me that he had plans for me that would prosper me and give me hope and a future. At that point I realized that, just as new wine should not be stored in old wine skins, my selfish and sinful dreams had to be completely deconstructed in order for God to reconstruct a new dream.

In my walk with him, God's dream was being reconstructed on top of the demolished site. What was being built on the Cornerstone was no longer a sinful and ambitious dream, but rather the dream that God had been dreaming for me before I was born. God was reconstructing the dream that he wanted to dream and build with me. Instead of my limited plans and pleasure-seeking mind, the Bible was the blueprint of his new dream. Instead of me, God himself was the architecture of the new dream. Instead of fulfilling my earthly and sinful pleasures, the new building project was established to please and glorify God. He is reconstructing the new construction for his glory. In Jesus, our destruction can be God's deconstruction to reconstruct his new construction.

God loves us. He has special dreams for us. Whatever they may be, they are good for us because they have been customized for us according to our character, past and future choices, and physical and spiritual condition. We may not like them and may want something else. However, his dreams are perfect for us and our lives will never be the same. There may be times when it is easy to believe in God's plans and love for us and praise him in joy, gratitude, and hope. But there will also be times of trials when he may seem far away from us and we may wonder whether he truly loves us or not and is almighty as the Bible indicates. There are times when our experience of suffering may seem more real than our experience of God's love. My friends, turn to the cross where he already demonstrated his love for you. Turn to the empty tomb where he no longer lies in his dead body but conquered the death once and for all in his glorious resurrection.

He loves us so much that he became like one of us, was humiliated in every way, experienced the very suffering that we have suffered, and gave his life for us. The Son of God who deserves nothing but honor and praise died like a notorious and wicked criminal on the cross, as if he legally and personally deserved it. His hands and feet were nailed to the tree; it took the whole weight of his body to deliver us from the very cross where we were to be crucified for our sins and guilt. His head was wounded by the crown of thorns in order to place on our head a crown more beautiful than the crown of David. His side was pierced by the spear where blood was poured out in order to deal with our sins, and water was poured out to give us new life which was dead in sin.

What appeared to be merely a story of the suffering and death of a historical figure was not the end of the story, but rather the beginning of the radical and scandalous story of the eternal God who was risen from the death on the third day. This resurrected Jesus was glorified in his physical body and he chose to stay on the earth for forty days. During this period he was seen, heard, touched, and experienced by many of his followers and by those who opposed him before ascending to heaven and sitting next to the Father in order to encourage future generations of believers to have hope in the very day when we will also be resurrected from death and receive a glorious body.

On that day, there will be no pain, disability, poverty, racism, discrimination, shame, fear, weakness, or suffering. The day will come when God will wipe our tears and heal our wounds. Until that day, let us hold our faith in Christ Jesus, strengthen each other to do so, and carry out God's plans for each one of us regardless of our hardship and challenges in love and humility, in partnership with our fellow brothers and sisters, and in the name that is above all names our Lord Jesus. Maranatha! Come, oh Lord Jesus come!

Made in the USA
Monee, IL
23 November 2024

71035475R00085